THE IMPLOSION OF CAPITALISM

THE IMPLOSION
OF CAPITALISM

Samir Amin

PlutoPress
www.plutobooks.com

First published in the UK 2014 by Pluto Press
345 Archway Road, London N6 5AA

www.plutobooks.com

British Library Cataloguing in Publication Data
A catalogue record for this book is available from the British Library

ISBN   978 0 7453 3453 0   Hardback
ISBN   978 0 7453 3452 3   Paperback
ISBN   978 1 7837 1001 0   PDF eBook
ISBN   978 1 7837 1003 4   Kindle eBook
ISBN   978 1 7837 1002 7   EPUB eBook

This book is printed on paper suitable for recycling and made from fully managed
and sustained forest sources. Logging, pulping and manufacturing processes are
expected to conform to the environmental standards of the country of origin.

10   9   8   7   6   5   4   3   2   1

Printed digitally by CPI Antony Rowe, Chippenham, UK

CONTENTS

PREFACE

HAVING ATTAINED THE CURRENT PHASE of its evolution, capitalism—the capitalism of generalized, financialized, and globalized monopolies; I will specify the significance of those adjectives further on—has nothing left to offer the human race but the lamentable perspective of self-destruction. Which is the ineluctable destination of its drive toward ever-extended capital accumulation. So capitalism is done for; it has laid the ground for conditions allowing us to envisage the necessary transition to a higher phase of civilization. The implosion of this system, resulting from its ongoing loss of control over its internal contradictions, by that very fact constitutes "the autumn of capitalism." But this autumn does not coincide with a "springtime of peoples." That would imply the workers and the struggling peoples having ascertained exactly what is needed, not to "emerge from the crisis of capitalism" but to "emerge from capitalism in crisis" (the title of one of my recent books). This is not, or not yet, the case.

The current historical moment, so dangerously dramatic, is fully characterized by the gap separating the autumn of capitalism from the possible springtime of peoples. The battle between the defenders of the capitalist order and those who, more than just resisting, are capable of embarking the human race on the long road to a socialism conceived as a higher phase of civilization—that battle has scarcely begun. So all the alternatives, the best as well as the most atrocious, remain possible.

The very existence of that gap needs to be explained. Capitalism is not merely a system based on the exploitation of labor by capital; it is just as much a system based on the polarized way in which it has been extended over the planet. Capitalism and imperialism, in their historic reality, are the two faces of a single coin. The system was called into question, over the whole twentieth century, until 1980, in the unfolding of a long wave of victorious struggles by workers and oppressed peoples. Revolutions carried out under the banners of Marxism and Communism, reforms won as steps in a gradual evolution toward socialism, victories by the national liberation movements of oppressed and colonized peoples—all these together shaped a balance of forces more favorable to the workers and the peoples than was previously the case. But that wave has petered out without reaching the point at which it would have established the conditions for further advances beyond its high-water mark. Its exhaustion then allowed monopoly capital to regain the offensive and to reestablish its unilateral and absolute power, whereas the outlines of the new wave that would again call the system into question had barely begun to be traced. Monsters and specters loom up before dawn in the dark twilight landscape of an uncompleted night. For even though generalized-monopoly capitalism's project is indeed monstrous, the replies from its rejecting forces remain mainly spectral.

Contemporary capitalism is a system based on false premises, according to which "markets" are self-regulating, whereas by their very nature they are explosive. Nevertheless, the forces contending with one another are so unbalanced that so stupid an idea was able to succeed. At times marked by a relative balance of contending forces, as was the case while the previous century's wave was still unfurling, the active forces in society are compelled to engage in intellectual development without which they cannot consolidate their gains. In contrast, an absolute imbalance rewards stupidity. Capital is allowed to imagine that it can forever do whatever it wants because historical development had reached its outer limits with the "definitive" defeat of socialism. The astounding mediocrity of our epoch's political class is a pale reflection of this stupidity bonus.

I have always believed, against the conventional wisdom, that this system is not viable. A study of the different aspects of its inexorable and ongoing implosion makes up the subject matter of this book: contradictions between a "growth policy" and the requirements of a financialization that the generalized monopolies find indispensable to their domination; implosion of a European system that is circumscribed by this form of globalization; the prospect of increasing conflicts between emerging countries and the world order; violent explosions of anger from the peoples condemned to undergo a "lumpen-development" model.

But this is not the whole story. The ongoing period is a time of chaotic transition (my 1991 book was titled *The Empire of Chaos*). The response of the victims—the workers and peoples confronting the destructive effects of the dominant system's implosion—remains far less than is required to meet the challenge. I do not believe that the challenge can possibly be met by putting forward ready-made formulas with one or another model of "twenty-first-century socialism." In contrast, I do believe it necessary and possible to trace the outlines of that boldness in thought and action without which there can be no rebirth of a radical left. In this book I advance several propositions to that end that are to be understood as contributions to a discussion about perspectives for the struggles that have already begun.

The Discourse about New Realities

There is indeed something new and important about the transformations in today's capitalism. They require the updating of our definitions and analyses concerning social classes, class struggles, political parties and social movements, the ideological forms in which these are expressed, and their ways of actively affecting social transformations. But the verbal formulae referring to that "something new"—postindustrial society, cybernetic revolution, the growth in production of "immaterial" or "nonmaterial" goods, the knowledge-based economy, the service society—all these remain vague. They need to be reexamined in the light of a critical perspective on capitalism.

Postindustrial Society or a New Stage in Global Industrialization?

To use the prefix "post," as in postcapitalist, postmodern, postindustrial, usually signifies an inability to give a precise characterization of the phenomenon under consideration. In a commonplace sense, the central countries (basically the United States, Europe, and Japan) seem indeed to be postindustrial societies. The percentages of the labor force engaged in material-transforming industries, and of the value-added contributed to nominal GDP by those industries, are plainly declining. But at the same time, in the major emerging peripheral countries (China, India, Brazil, and others), similar manufacturing industries are growing at an accelerated rate. It even seems that the two proportions referred to above are growing there, even though there is still only modest growth in the proportion of the labor force in industry. The growth rate is even more modest where emergence is linked to a mode of lumpen-development and still more so when the so-called development process is limited to that mode.

Thus, on the world-system scale, an exact estimation of this possible "postindustrial" evolution remains to be done. And even were it to be done this simple description of the recorded facts would require an explanation that those who use this phrase fail to supply. I will return below to the hypotheses which I offer about this.

Classes or Social Categories?
Class Struggles or Social Movements?

The fashionable thing, in discussing postindustrial society, is hurriedly to declare that the concepts of class and of class struggle are "outmoded." It is then suggested (for example by the sociologist Alain Touraine) that the Marxist (and therefore outmoded) traditional vision of class struggle, particularly of struggle between the proletariat and the bourgeoisie, is to be replaced with struggle, primarily directed against the state, by activist militants in the social movements.

Here again, and even if one might feel that empirical facts give a measure of credibility to the description at issue, there would still be no explanation of why such is the case. Touraine and the rest offer only a tautological account: things are that way because modern postindustrial society is marked by the fragmentation of waged labor, status differentiations in regard to skills and working conditions, the prevalence of individualism, etc. These characteristics, linked to changes in organization of production that are themselves results of technological revolutions (especially cybernetics), are supposed to have wiped out the broad inclusive classes, like the proletariat of the industrial period, and replaced them with an ever-increasing number of "social categories" that express their ambitions in ways as diverse as those categories themselves. For its part individualism raises The Citizen, or a generic category (women), or a community (immigrants from some given country) to the rank of transformative social actors. It goes with the adoption of a new stance within social movements that renounces the strategic objective of conquering power as the means of social transformation, replacing it with individualized goals tending to reduce the power of the state in favor of power exercised directly by "civil society."

All of this is seemingly evident: these phenomena are there to be seen. But these realities are themselves problematic. For example, the question that needs to be asked about the fragmentation of labor and the conditions in which it is carried out is whether it necessarily results from technological revolutions, or whether it stems from strategies whereby capital turns those revolutions to its profit. In regard to the prevalence of individualism, the question is whether the space it opens for the individuals involved to act freely is really what they imagine it to be, or, if that is not the case (which as well seems to be a recognizable fact), how and why the ideology of individualism has come to prevail. And a complementary question: What is the real distance between the things that can be transformed through the progress of social movements and the things that cannot be transformed without the transformation of state power itself?

Nonmaterial Production, Service Society, or Generalized-Monopoly Capitalism?

Here again we must go beyond mere recognition of facts: the undeniable growth in the type of production clumsily called "immaterial" by some, more correctly "nonmaterial" (output of services) by others. This is incontestably the case in regard to the advanced and dominant capitalist centers. But it is more doubtful in regard to the peripheries, which are marked by the growth of activities that seem equally nonmaterial but whose nature is of a very different sort from that characteristic of the transformations in the centers. Although material outputs—defined as those produced by transforming physically existing raw materials, by means of equally visible equipment, in order to fabricate completed physical products—make up, despite their diversity, a homogeneous whole (all corresponding to this definition), such is not the case with nonmaterial outputs. Activities of a profoundly different nature are being linked all too casually. For some of these services are, by their very nature, directly articulated with material production. For example, transportation of and commerce in material products, or financial activities servicing material production and the services involved with it. But other "immaterial" products are not related, or only distantly related, to material production. For example, general education—as distinct from training directly needed to make available the requisite supply of specifically skilled workers—or, even more so, health care.

The relation between the equipment needed for such diverse nonmaterial activities and the workers using it is diversified among the categories of nonmaterial production involved. The equipment (infrastructure, vehicles, and the like) needed for transportation, or buildings and inventories for commerce, is related to the direct labor of workers in transportation and commerce in which equipment and direct labor are related in material production. Contrariwise, a teacher's computer and a doctor's sophisticated apparatus are not the kind of equipment similar to those. In these cases the equipment (products of indirect labor) are complements to the direct labor of the teacher or doctor, not substitutes for direct labor as is the case with advanced mechanization in a factory. To amalgamate all these "immaterial" outputs, which indeed have always existed, and then draw the simple conclusion that they are growing much faster than material output, is scarcely satisfactory for anyone who wants to know why, and to what extent, things are that way.

This question—the comparative growth rates of material and nonmaterial outputs—cannot be considered apart from those concerning their articulation and functioning within the capitalist system as a whole. For my part, I have tried to reestablish that linkage—which is ignored in postmodernist chatter. Doing so, I emphasized two distinct series of questions. First of all, about the growing surplus generated by the workings of monopoly capitalism and about its absorption through the growth of a third department in addition to the two departments of Marx's model in volume 2 of *Capital*. Secondly, about the social utility of certain nonmaterial activities both in capitalist society and—even more so—in the socialist project of building a society with a more advanced civilization. The arguments dealing with these two questions will be taken up further on.

The fact remains that in capitalist society the social substance of both material and nonmaterial production is to be found in the amount of social labor time expended to obtain any given product, whether material or nonmaterial. And insofar as the reward for labor (basically wage-labor) is identical (or comparable) in all these productive activities as they are performed in developed-center capitalism—that is, compensated with a wage corresponding to a set of goods and services costing for their output a lesser quantity of labor time than that provided by the worker involved— all such material and nonmaterial activities are part of the production of surplus-value (as defined by Marx) and thereby are productive of profit.

And yet the measurement of social labor's productivity in some types of nonmaterial production is subject to certain difficulties and uncertainties peculiar to that activity. In material production, at least in the short term, any improvement in the productivity of social labor can be easily measured: so many meters of cotton fabric produced today using a lesser amount of (direct and indirect) social labor as against the labor needed to produce that many meters yesterday. But how to measure the productivity of a teacher's or doctor's labor—by the number of students or of patients? Or by the quality of the results? In capitalism, nevertheless, all nonmaterial activities that have been privatized do indeed have a productivity that is manifest to the capital managing their production: the profit that can be derived from them. But in such a case the productivity is purely private and can conflict with the social productivity of the activity at issue, as against material production in which case private and social productivities are conflated.

The apparent growth of nonmaterial activities is inseparable from the evolution of the division of labor. As soon as the conception of, design of, and/or control over the market are externalized—that is, carried out by other firms than those providing a given material or nonmaterial product—nonmaterial production is inflated by that very externalization. In general, externalization as carried out by a firm turns some elements of its output into subcontracted services.

What is more, growth in the dominant centers' nonmaterial activities is inseparable from how the division of labor is unequally shared between centers and peripheries. That material production is outsourced to the peripheries aggravates, in the centers, the growth of the nonmaterial activities involved in controlling it—for example, by concentration in the centers of the means of control over technologies, of globalized finance, and of communications.

Postmodernist talk about a postcapitalist service society is linked to fashionable arguments about a so-called cognitive economy, in which scientific knowledge and technological mastery are supposedly divorced from direct labor and have become factors of production in their own right. Marx, contrariwise, unifies (and doesn't dissociate) the different dimensions of the single reality that is social labor, and he conceptualizes its productivity quite differently. Social labor applies to its work the special and general forms of knowledge that lets its productivity be what it is. We need only recall how important Marx considered the "general intellect" to be in this regard. The economy has forever been "cognitive" because, even among the most "primitive" of prehistoric hunter-gatherers, production has always involved the application of existing knowledge. Granted, the forms of knowledge now applied in production are infinitely more advanced than those required in past forms of production, even in the near past of nineteenth-century industry. But even that obvious fact allows no in-depth understanding until these questions have been answered: who governs the development of knowledge in contemporary society? How are those parts of knowledge serviceable to capital chosen and used?

I believe that I have not failed to take into account the realities described above. Nor have I limited myself to critique of the dominant discourse about them. I have attempted to go further, to integrate them into an overall analysis, which is the only way to situate them, to give them their rightful place. The analysis in which the totality of these phenomena coheres has as its central axis what I call generalized-monopoly capitalism. To analyze it is the aim of this book.

1. CAPITALISM IN THE AGE OF GENERALIZED MONOPOLIES

CONTEMPORARY CAPITALISM IS A CAPITALISM of generalized monopolies. By this I mean that monopolies are now no longer islands in a sea of other still relatively autonomous companies, but are constitutive of an integrated system. Therefore, these monopolies now tightly control all the systems of production. Small and medium enterprises, and even the large corporations that are not strictly speaking oligopolies, are locked in a network of control put in place by the monopolies. Their degree of autonomy has shrunk to the point that they are nothing more than subcontractors of the monopolies. This system of generalized monopolies is the product of a new phase of centralization of capital in the countries of the Triad—the United States, Western and Central Europe, and Japan—that took place during the 1980s and 1990s. The generalized monopolies now dominate the world economy. "Globalization" is the name they have given to the set of demands by which they exert their control over the productive systems of the periphery of global capitalism (the world beyond the partners of the Triad). It is nothing other than a new stage of imperialism.

This capitalism of generalized and globalized monopolies is a system that guarantees these monopolies a monopoly rent levied on the mass of surplus-value (transformed into profits) that capital extracts from the exploitation of labor. To the extent that these monopolies are operating in the peripheries of the global system, monopoly rent is imperialist rent. The process of capital accumulation, which defines capitalism in all its successive historical forms, is therefore driven by the maximization of monopoly/imperialist rent-seeking. This shift in the center of gravity of the accumulation of capital is the source of the continuous concentration of income and wealth to the benefit of the monopolies, largely monopolized by the oligarchies (plutocracies) that govern oligopolistic groups, at the expense of the remuneration of labor and even the remuneration of non-monopolistic capital.

This imbalance in continued growth is, in turn, the source of the financialization of the economic system. By this I mean that a growing portion of the surplus cannot be invested in the expansion and deepening of systems of production, and therefore the "financial investment" of this excessive surplus becomes the only option for continued accumulation under the control of the monopolies.

The implementation of specific systems by capital permits the financialization to operate in different ways:

1. Subjugation of the management of firms to the principle of "shareholder value";
2. Substitution of pension systems funded by personal saving and capitalization (pension funds) for systems of pension distribution paid by current taxation (transfer payments);
3. Adoption of the principle of flexible exchange rates;
4. Abandonment of the principle of central banks determining the interest rate—the price of liquidity—and the transfer of this responsibility to the market.

Financialization has transferred the major responsibility for control of the reproduction of the system of accumulation to some thirty giant banks of the Triad. What are euphemistically called "markets" are nothing other than places where the strategies of these actors who dominate the economic scene are deployed. In turn, this financialization, which is responsible for the growth of inequality in income distribution (and fortunes), generates the growing surplus on which it feeds. The "financial investments," or rather the investments in financial speculation, continue to grow at dizzying speeds, not commensurate with growth in GDP (which is therefore becoming largely fictitious) or with investment in real production. Among other things, the explosive growth of financial investment requires, and fuels, debt in all its forms, especially sovereign debt. When the governments in power claim to be pursuing the goal of debt reduction, they are deliberately lying. The strategy of financialized monopolies requires the growth in debt, which they seek rather than combat, as a way to absorb the surplus profit of monopolies. The austerity policies imposed to reduce debt have indeed resulted, as intended, in increasing its volume.

It is this system—commonly called neoliberal, the system of generalized monopoly capitalism, globalized (imperialist) and financialized (of necessity for its own reproduction)—that is imploding before our eyes. This system, apparently unable to overcome its growing internal contradictions, is doomed to continue its wild ride. The crisis of the system is due to its own success. Indeed, so far the strategy deployed by monopolies has always produced the desired results: austerity plans and the so-called social (in fact antisocial) downsizing plans that are still being imposed, in spite of resistance and struggles. To this day the initiative remains in the hands of the monopolies, "the markets," and their political servants—the governments that submit to the demands of the so-called "market."

In this analytic perspective of monopoly-capitalism's transformation, it seems necessary to reformulate the theory of surplus (a distinct concept from that of surplus-value) and, by extending its field of action to the global system, to unveil the nature of the monopoly rent/imperialist rent that has come to exert a unilateral dictatorship over the accumulation process on a world scale.

Beyond Surplus-Value: The Concept of Surplus

The surplus at issue is the result of growth in the productivity of social labor exceeding that of the price paid for labor power. Let us assume, for example, that the rate of growth in the productivity of social labor is about 4.5 percent per year, sufficient to double the net product over a period of about fifteen years, corresponding to an assumed average lifetime for capital equipment.

Let us assume that, in the long run, real wages would grow at a rate of about 2.5 percent per year to bring about an increase of 40 percent over a fifteen-year span. At the end of a half-century's regular and continuous evolution of the system, the surplus (which defines the size of Department

III relative to net revenue, itself the sum of wages, reinvested profits, and surplus) takes up two-thirds of the net product, roughly equivalent to GDP. The shift indicated here is approximately what happened during the twentieth century in the "developed" centers of world capitalism (the United States/Europe/Japan Triad).

Analysis of the components corresponding to the concept of surplus shows the diversity of the regulations governing their administration.

Corresponding approximately to Marx's Departments I and II in the national accounts are the sectors defined respectively as "primary" (agricultural production and mining), "secondary" (manufacturing), and a portion of so-called tertiary activities that are hard to derive from statistics that were not designed for that purpose, even when the definition of their status is not itself confusing. To be held to participate—indirectly—in the output of Departments I and II are transportation of implements, raw materials, and finished products; trade in those products; and the cost of managing the financial institutions needed to service the two departments. What are not to be regarded as direct or indirect constitutive elements in their output, and therefore counted as elements of surplus, are government administration, public expenditures and transfer payments (for education, health, social security, pensions, and old-age benefits), services (advertising) corresponding to selling costs, and personal services paid for out of income (including housing). Whether the "services" at issue, lumped together in the national accounts under the title "tertiary activities" (with the possibility of distinguishing among them a new sector termed "quaternary"), are administered by public or private entities does not by itself qualify them as belonging to Department III: the surplus. The fact remains that the volume of tertiary activities in the developed countries of the center (as in many of the peripheral countries, though that question—a different one—does not concern us here) is much larger than that of the primary and secondary sector. Moreover, the sum of taxes and obligatory contributions in those countries by itself amounts to or exceeds 40 percent of their GDP. Talk by some fundamentalist right-wing ideologists calling for "reduction" of these fiscal extractions is purely demagogic: capitalism can no longer function in any other way. In reality, any possible decrease in the taxes paid by the "rich" must necessarily be made up by heavier taxation on the "poor."

We can thus estimate without risk of major error that the surplus (Department III) accounts for half of GDP or, in other terms, has grown from 10 percent of GDP in the nineteenth century to 50 percent in the first decade of the twenty-first century. So if in Marx's day an analysis of accumulation limited to consideration of Departments I and II made sense, that is no longer the case. The enrichment of Marxist thought by Baran, Sweezy, and Magdoff through their taking account of Department III and the linked concept of "surplus," defined as we have recalled it, is for that reason decisive. I find it deplorable that this is still doubted by a majority of the analysts of contemporary Marxism.

Once again, not everything in this surplus is to be condemned as useless or parasitical. Far from it! On the contrary, growth in a large fraction of the expenditures linked to Department III is worthy of support. For a more advanced stage in the unfolding of human civilization, spending on such activities as education, health care, social security, and retirement—or even other socializing services linked to democratic forms of structuring alternatives to structuring by the market, such as public transport, housing, and others—would be summoned to take on even more importance. In contrast, some constitutive elements of Department III—like the "selling costs" that grew so fabulously during the twentieth century—are evidently of a parasitic nature and were viewed early on as such by some economists, like Joan Robinson, who were then minimized or disparaged by their profession. Some public expenditures (weapons) and some private (security guards, legal departments) likewise are parasitic. A fraction of Department III, to be sure, is (or should we say was?) made up of spending that benefits workers and complements their wages (health care, unemployment insurance, pensions). Just the same, these benefits, won by the working classes through intense struggle, have been called into question during the past three decades, some have been cut back severely, others have shifted from provision by a public authority based on the principle of social solidarity to private management supposedly "freely bargained for" on the basis of "individual rights." This management technique, prevalent in the United States and expanding in Europe, opens supplementary and very lucrative areas for the investment of surplus.

The fact remains that in capitalism all these usages of the GDP—whether "useful" or not—fulfill the same function: to allow accumulation to continue despite the growing insufficiency of labor incomes. What is more, the permanent battle over transferring many fundamental elements of Department III from public to private management opens supplemental opportunities for capital to make a profit (and thereby increase the volume of surplus). Private medical care tells us that if the sick are to be treated it must above all be profitable—to private clinics, to laboratories, to pharmaceutical manufacturers, and to the insurers. My analysis of Department III of surplus absorption stands within the spirit of the pioneering work of Baran and Sweezy. The necessary conclusion is that a large proportion of the activities managed on those terms are parasitic and inflate the GDP, thus reducing drastically its significance as an indicator of the real wealth of a society.

Counterposed to this is the current fashion of considering the rapid growth of Department III as a sign of the transformation of capitalism, its passage from the Industrial Age into a new stage, the "Knowledge Economy." Capital's unending pursuit of realization would thus regain its legitimacy. The expression "knowledge capitalism" is itself an oxymoron. Tomorrow's economy, the socialist economy, would indeed be a "knowledge economy," but capitalism can never be such. To fantasize that the development of the productive forces is establishing—within capitalism—tomorrow's economy, as the writings of Antonio Negri and his students would have us believe, has only a seeming validity. In reality, the realization of capital, necessarily based on the oppression of labor, wipes out the progressive aspect of this development. This annihilation is at the core of the development of Department III, designed to absorb the surplus inseparable from monopoly capitalism.

We must therefore avoid confounding today's reality (capitalism) with a fantasy about the future (socialism). Socialism is not a more adequate form of capitalism, doing the same things but only better and with a fairer income distribution. However, its governing paradigm—socialization of management over direct production of use-values—thus comports exactly with a powerful development of some of the expenditures that currently, under capitalism, take part in its main function, surplus absorption.

In its globalized setup capitalism is inseparable from imperialist exploitation of its dominated peripheries by its dominant centers. Under monopoly capitalism this exploitation takes the form of monopoly rents (in ordinary language, the superprofits of multinational corporations) that are by and large imperialist rents.

The order of magnitude of the quantifiable fraction of the imperialist rent, the result of the differential in the prices of labor powers of equal productivity, is obviously large. In order to give a sense of that order of magnitude, we hypothesize a division of the world's Gross Product in the ratio of two-thirds for the centers (20 percent of the world's population) and one-third for the peripheries (80 percent of the population). We assume an annual rate of growth of Gross Product of 4.5 percent for both centers and peripheries, and a rate of growth of wages of 3.5 percent for the centers but total stagnation (zero growth) for peripheral wages. After fifteen years of development in this model we would arrive at the following result: the imperialist rent would be on the order of half the Gross Domestic Product of the peripheries, or 17 percent of the world's Gross Product and 25 percent of the centers' GDPs.

Of course, the volume of this imperialist rent is partially hidden by exchange rates. It is a question here of a well-known reality that introduces uncertainty into international comparisons—are GDP value-comparisons to be made in terms of market exchange rates or according to exchange rates reflecting purchasing-power parities? Moreover, the rent is not transferred as a net benefit to the centers. That the local ruling classes hold on to some of it is the condition for their agreement to "play the globalization game." But the fact remains that the material benefits drawn from this rent, accruing not only to the profit of capital ruling on a world scale but equally to the profit of the centers' opulent societies, are more than considerable.

In addition to the quantifiable advantages linked to differential pricing of labor powers, there are others, nonquantifiable but no less crucial, based on exclusive access to the planet's material resources, on technological monopolies, and on control over the globalized financial system.

The share of imperialist rent transferred from the peripheries to the centers accentuates in its turn the global disequilibrium pointed out by Baran and forms an additional factor swelling the surplus to be absorbed. The contrast to be observed during the present phase of the crisis, between weak growth in the centers (United States, Europe, Japan) and rapid growth in the developing countries of the periphery, is to be understood only in terms of an overall analysis linking how surplus is absorbed to the extraction of imperialist rent.

Simple Labor, Complex Labor, Abstract Labor

The unit of abstract labor, whether an hour or a year of abstract social labor, is a composite unit combining units of simple (unskilled) and complex (skilled) labor in some given proportion.

Let us choose a sample of one hundred workers distributed among the different categories of (differently skilled) workers in exactly similar proportions to their distribution in the overall society (whose labor force, for example, might number thirty million). In the following simplified analysis we take account of only two categories of labor: (1) Simple labor involves only 60 percent of the sample (sixty workers); (2) complex labor involves 40 percent of the sample (forty workers).

We assume that each year the workers in the sample provide the same annual number of labor hours—say, 8 hours per day and 220 days per year. Thus in each year a simple (unskilled) worker contributes one year of simple labor to the collective social labor, while a skilled worker provides a contribution to one year of complex labor. We abstract from the cost of training simple workers because this training is that which is provided to all citizens. Contrariwise, we take into consideration the cost of supplementary training for skilled workers. The latter, for example, would extend for ten years and for each of those years would cost, for each worker involved, the equivalent of two years of social labor to cover the cost of teachers, training equipment, and the student's living expenses.

Whereas the unskilled worker would work for thirty years, the skilled one would work for only twenty years, having devoted the first ten years to being trained. The cost of this training (twenty years of social labor) would be recovered over twenty years of this labor through the valorization of complex labor. In other words, the unit of complex labor (an hour or a year) would be worth two units of simple labor.

It follows that 60 percent of a composite unit of abstract labor would consist of the equivalent of one unit of simple labor, and 40 percent of the equivalent of one unit of complex labor (worth two units of simple labor). In other words, *one unit of abstract labor provided by the labor collective is worth 1.4 units of simple labor.*

I call attention to the following points:

1. The value of a commodity is to be measured according to the quantity of abstract labor required for its production because none of the workers work in isolation; he is nothing apart from the team in which he is a part. Production is collective, and the productivity of labor is that of the social labor collective, not that of team members taken separately one from the other.

2. I have not introduced into my argument the scale of real wages received by each category of workers, only the cost of their training, which is the sole "price" paid by the society to dispose of the labor force appropriate to its productions.

Production of Surplus-Value, Consumption of Surplus-Value

The value of the team's annual production and the measure of the extraction of a surplus-value on this occasion are calculated in quantities of abstract labor.

Under point 1, and for our team of 100 workers, we assume that the real wage given to each skilled worker is double that of a simple worker, this relationship being that of the value of an hour of complex labor to that of an hour of simple labor. It is easy to recognize that the wage for a skilled worker is double that for an unskilled worker, as the former contributes twice as much to the value of the product as does the latter. Both equally contribute to the extraction of surplus-value, in the same proportion. The rate of surplus-value here is 100 percent. For an hour of labor provided by a simple worker, he receives a wage allowing him to buy consumption goods whose value is equal to one half-hour of abstract labor. Each labor-hour provided by a skilled worker is worth twice as much and likewise his wage is twice as large, allowing him to buy consumption goods whose value is equal to one hour of abstract labor.

We now take a wage-scale different from that which would imply an equality between the wage and the contribution to the formation of value. In this second hypothesis the wage retained by a skilled worker is four times (rather than double) that of a simple worker. Under this hypothesis, then, we recognize that only unskilled workers contribute to the formation of surplus-value; the skilled workers "devour" the surplus-value to whose formation they contribute.

It then is quite clear that if the wage-scale for the various categories of skilled labor has a broad extent, going, say, from 1.5 to 2 times the subsistence minimum wage (the wage for unskilled labor) for many, three to four times as much for some and much more for a tiny (extra-skilled) minority, we would recognize that if the majority of workers contribute to the formation of surplus-value, although in different proportions—and this gives its full meaning to the term "super-exploited" for the majority, two-thirds, of the workers—there exists a category of the supposed "extra-skilled" (who may sometimes actually be so) who consume more surplus-value than what they contribute to its formation.

Some Reflections

In Marx's analysis there exists only one "productivity," that of social labor defined by "the quantities" of abstract labor contained in the commodity produced by a collective of workers. Bourgeois economic theory attempts to prove that the mode of decision making in the framework of its system of prices and incomes produces a rational allocation of labor and capital resources synonymous with an optimum pattern of output. But it can reach that goal only through cascading tautological arguments. To do so it artificially slices productivity into "components" attributed to "factors of production." Although this pattern of slices has no scientific value and rests only on tautological argument, it is "useful" because it is the only way to legitimize capital's profits. The operative method of this bourgeois economics to determine "the wage" by the marginal productivity of "the last employee hired" stems from the same tautology and breaks up the unity of the collective, the sole creator of value. Moreover, contrary to the unproven affirmations of conventional economics, employers do not make decisions by using such marginal calculations.

The wage-scale under real capitalism is not determined by the cost of training skilled workers. It is broadly larger and has no other explanation except through considering the history of concrete social formations and class struggles. Its attempted legitimization through the "marginal productivities" of the contributions of different categories of workers is tautological.

The fundamental inequality in capitalism's characteristic distribution of income rests primarily on the contrast opposing the power of capital-owners to the subordination of labor-power sellers. The wage-scale comes as an addition to that. But this wage-scale has by now acquired a new dimension. The contemporary capitalist system of generalized monopolies is based on an extreme centralization of control over capital, accompanied by a generalization of wage-labor. In these conditions a large fraction of profit is disguised in the form of the "wages" (or quasi-wages) of the higher layers of the "middle classes" whose activities are those of the servants of capital. The separation among the formation of value, the extraction of surplus-value, and its distribution has become wider.

We now have the means to grasp how social structures are being transformed, which I term the diversification of the "generalized proletariat."

The Financial Oligarchy and Generalized Proletarianization

The formation of generalized-monopoly capitalism resulted in structural transformation both of the dominant and the dominated classes. In the dominant centers, social polarization has taken on an extreme form: opposition between a financial oligarchy, supported by new middle classes, and an agglomeration of dominated classes made up of segments whose diverse statuses belie their common inclusion in what I call a generalized proletariat. In the peripheral countries, the forms of polarization differ according to whether the country is, or is not, in emergence.

The logic of accumulation is the logic of an ever-growing concentration and centralization of control over capital. I count as crucial this distinction between property in, and control over, capital. Formal property ownership might be widespread, as with workers having a right to retirement benefits from "their" pension funds, but how that property is managed is under the control of finance capital.

Competition—whose virtues, both real and imaginary, are extolled by the system's ideology—remains. But now the competitors are no more than an ever-dwindling number of oligopolies. It is a competition that is neither "perfect" nor even "open." Such competition has never existed, and, as really existing capitalism develops, its workings resemble such competition less and less.

We have now been brought to a degree of centralization of capital's dominating powers such that all hitherto known forms of the bourgeoisie's existence and organization have been abolished. The bourgeoisie used to be made up of stable bourgeois families. From one generation to another, their heirs maintained a certain specialization in the business of their firms. The bourgeoisie built, and constructed itself, in a long-term perspective. That stability promoted confidence in "bourgeois values," and facilitated their extension throughout society. To a very great extent the position of the bourgeoisie as dominant class was generally accepted. In return for services rendered to society, the bourgeoisie seemed entitled to their privileged access to comfort, even to wealth. The bourgeoisie appeared as a class within the nation, motivated by the national interest, whatever the ambiguities and limitations of that manipulated concept. Now the new ruling class has broken abruptly with that tradition. Some term this transformation a mobilization of activist shareholders fully reestablishing the rights of proprietors (and even of working-class shareholders). This is a deceptive, fulsome legitimization of the change, concealing the fact that the most important aspects of the transformation involve the degree of centralization of power and of control over capital inherent in it.

Assuredly, large-scale concentration of capital is no new thing. At the end of the nineteenth century, what Hilferding, Hobson, and Lenin termed monopoly capitalism was already a reality. Certainly this concentration was—and has continuously been—more advanced in the United States than in the other capitalist centers. In the United States the formation of very large, incipiently transnational, corporations had begun before the Second World War and expanded without resistance afterward; Europe followed in its footsteps. Just as assuredly, the American ideology of the "self-made man," à la John D. Rockefeller or Henry Ford, is a clear break with European familial conservatism. As also the cult of "true" competition, even where such competition was nonexistent, which is why antitrust laws were passed as early as 1890. But irrespective of these real differences in their political cultures, there prevails the same transformation in the mode of existence of capitalism's new ruling class in Europe as in the United States.

The new ruling class is counted by the tens of thousands and no longer, like the old bourgeoisie, by the millions. What is more, a large fraction of this class is made up of parvenus who rose much more by successful financial (notably stock market) operations than by any contribution to our epoch's technological breakthroughs. Their ultra-rapid rise contrasts with the protracted, generations-long ascent of their forerunners. Likewise, the appearance of a swarm of "startups" points to a new characteristic—extreme instability leading to failure for nearly all of these naïve upstarts, despite the thoughtless laudatory rhetoric about them.

Centralization of political power is even more striking than concentration of capital. It accentuates the interpenetration of economic and political power. Once again, there is nothing new in this. After all, the class nature of political power—democratic or not—means that the governing elite is at the service of capital. As payback, the great capitalist fortunes have always invited some among the governing politicians to share in their emoluments. But henceforward this interpenetration became a virtual homogenization, and that is new. It is expressed in the transformations of capitalism's ideological discourse.

Capitalism's "traditional" ideology emphasized the virtues of property as such, especially for small (in reality mid- or medium-large-sized) enterprises. They were regarded, thanks to their stability, as the bringers of social and technological progress. In contrast, the new ideology worships "winners" and has only unconditional contempt for the "losers." The dominant rhetoric paints an illusory image of success, the better to ascribe the losers' failures to their personal circumstances and in that way absolve the social system of its responsibility. Do we really have to point out that this ideology—evoking a sort of Social Darwinism (the reference to Darwin being quite wrong, as Anton Pannekoek and many others have pointed out)—is close to that of the Mafia? For the "winner" is scarcely ever wrong, though his methods, even when not technically illegal, border on illegality, and in any case has no regard for established moral values.

A concrete illustration of this harsh judgment is the collusion of the business world with its audit and rating institutions, with the at least tacit complicity of governmental regulatory institutions. Those agencies, in the pay of the monopolies, pose as arbiters standing above all others with exclusive power to set the rules of the game, the bounds beyond which democracy itself is forbidden to step! To pay the least attention to such agencies is to capitulate. A leftist policy worthy of the name has to throw any ratings by those agencies into the trash can. Then the problem can be posed as it should be in a democracy: how to define the conflicting social interests, how to frame propositions of a social compromise that would enjoy broad popular support, how to impose its provisions on monopoly capital.

It is said that the particular way in which enterprises are financed in the United States, their resort to the financial market for the issuance of equity and debt certificates rather than to banks and/or specialized governmental institutions, is at the origin of such a conjunction. This is true in part. But the fact remains that the German and Japanese models favoring financial integration between banks and corporations, as well as the French model based on partial capital ownership by the state and by state-owned financial institutions, have not kept these systems from being swept up in the same ongoing evolution. This is so because the basic logic of this evolution stems from the high level of centralization and control over capital, incomparably greater than it was a mere three decades ago. The collusion between economic and political power, fusing to become a single power, recalls what Marx and Braudel said of capitalism: that it cannot be reduced to the "market," as the dominant discourse reiterates *ad nauseam*. The opposite is true: capitalism finds its identity in oligopolies and the state, powers "above the market." In the "new capitalism," this collusion, which was far weaker during the eighteenth and nineteenth centuries, now operates as forcefully as it did at the very beginnings of capitalism—when the republic of Venice was run as a joint-stock company owned by the richest merchants—or in the "Elizabethan" or "Colbertian" epochs of absolute monarchy. Which, by itself, bears witness that the system really has become obsolete, has entered its senility.

By force of the logic of accumulation, contemporary capitalism has become a "collusive capitalism." The English term "crony capitalism" can no longer be applied only to its "underdeveloped and corrupt" South Asian and Latin-American forms, which the economists, sincere and convinced believers in the virtues of liberalism, were denouncing only yesterday. It applies equally well to contemporary American and European capitalism. In its current behavior this ruling class closely approaches that of the Mafia, however insulting and extreme that term might be felt to be. The "system" has no response to this deviance, because it quite simply is unable to call into question the centralization of capital. The measures it takes strangely resemble the American nineteenth-century antitrust laws like the Sherman Act, whose ineffectiveness is known to all.

Longer term, a new regroupment of the radical European left pursuant to its political culture would obviously be able to challenge this setup and its accompanying deviance. But that probably could not be done without in the process challenging capitalism itself in some of its essential attributes. Democratic breakthroughs that would make possible such a recomposition of the left would challenge the established models of centralized oligarchic power. The European left, alas, has not taken this road.

Contemporary capitalism's preferred political system, henceforward, is plutocracy, which easily goes along with continuation of representative democratic institutions in what has become a "low-intensity democracy": you are free to vote for whomever you want, because your choice has no importance. It is the market, not the representative assembly, that decides everything. The market gets along just as well with autocratic political regimes as it does with those designated by an electoral farce.

These transformations altered both the status of the middle classes and the modalities of their integration into the overall system. These middle classes are now mainly composed of wage workers, no longer of small commodity producers. This transformation has taken on crisis proportions for the increasingly diversified middle classes. Their privileged and highly paid members have become direct agents of the oligopolistic ruling class, with the rest becoming impoverished. Earlier in this chapter, in my analysis of the division of (mainly hired) workers between those who consume and those who produce surplus-value, I suggested a way in which to identify those "layers" of the middle class that form part of the dominant social coalition.

The Corruptionists: A New Ruling Class in the Peripheries

The contrast between central and peripheral countries is not a new one; it was present in globalized capitalist expansion in its very origins, five centuries ago. Whether in independent countries or in colonies, the local ruling classes in capitalism's peripheral lands have always had subaltern status. Nevertheless, they were allies of the capitalist center, thanks to the profits deriving from their role within the globalized capitalist system.

There is considerable diversity among those classes, which generally descend from the classes that dominated those societies before their subordination to capitalism/imperialism. They have undergone equally considerable transformations stemming from their subaltern integration: former political chiefs became great landed proprietors, modernized former aristocracies, etc. Regained independence often involved replacement of those former collaborating subordinate classes by new ruling classes—bureaucracies, state bourgeoisies—that originally seemed more legitimate to their peoples thanks to their association with national liberation movements.

Even so, the local ruling classes in those peripheral countries dominated by the former imperialism (the pre-1950 model) or by the new imperialism (from Bandung to about 1980) clearly enjoyed a relative stability. For a long time the successive generations of aristocrats and neo-bourgeois, and then the new generation sprung from political forces brought to power by national liberations, at least adhered to some moral or national value-system, which endowed the men (and occasionally the women) representing those generations with some, though varying, degrees of legitimacy.

The former ruling classes in the periphery found their power uprooted by the upheavals that the oligopoly capitalism of the new collective imperialist center (the United States/Europe/Japan Triad) brought about. In their place, power passed to a new class that I term "corruptionists," a label that spontaneously has become current in many countries of the South. The corruptionist is a "businessman," not a creative entrepreneur. He draws his wealth from his associations with the established political power holders and the foreign masters of the system—the representatives (especially the CIA) of the imperialist states or of the oligopolies. He operates as a highly compensated intermediary, profiting from an actual political rent that is the essential source of his accumulated wealth. The corruptionist adheres to no system of national or moral values whatsoever. A caricatured image of his counterparts in the dominant centers, he recognizes only "success," only money, only greed—barely screened by his praise for a supposed "individuality." His behavior, likewise, is never far from that of a mafioso or a gangster.

This sort of phenomenon is not altogether novel. The very nature of imperialist domination over submissive local ruling classes favored the emergence of this sort of power broker. But what is certainly new is that these types have now taken over virtually the whole domain of power and wealth. They are "friends," the only friends, of the world's ruling plutocracy. But their power is fragile, because their people regard them as having no legitimacy whatsoever—not from traditional status, nor from participation in national liberation. This is the framework for what has been called the "crisis of the middle classes" in the peripheral countries.

The formation of this new corruptionist class is inextricably implicated in the extension of forms of lumpen-development to cover most of today's global South. But the central element of the dominant coalition is made up of this class only in the situation in which its country is not emergent. The dominant coalition in the emergent countries is of a different sort.

I will attempt, further on, to specify the conditions for emergence and to show the possible combinations between emergence and the extension of pauperization involved in what I call lumpen-development. The dominant social coalitions in peripheral countries are not merely, as they have always been, specific to each country; they differ insofar as the country is or is not emergent. Political governance itself is different in emergent and non-emergent countries. In the emergent countries there is a real state power, and its commitment to a project (whatever its limitations) of social transformation endows these regimes with some legitimacy. But legitimacy has been destroyed where the country remains entirely under the sway of imperialist capital. There we have comprador states, complementing their comprador bourgeoisies.

The Subordinate Classes: A Generalized but Segmented Proletariat

Marx gave a rigorous definition of the proletarian (a human being constrained to sell his labor power to capital) and recognized the diversity of conditions under which that sale—"formal" or "real," in Marx's terminology—has always taken place. There is nothing new about segmentation of the proletariat. It is understood that for some segments of the working class—workers in the new machine industries of the nineteenth century or, better yet, workers in the "Fordist" factories of the twentieth—their skilled status was more visible than for others. Their concentration around the workplace facilitated their solidarity in struggle and the maturation of their political consciousness, but it also fed into the trade-unionist outlook characterizing certain historical forms of Marxism. Today, the fragmentation of production resulting from capital's strategy of using all the possibilities of modern technology while keeping control over subcontracted or outsourced production has, of course, weakened working-class solidarity and accentuated the class's perception of a diversity of interests within itself.

The proletariat thus seems to disappear at the very moment when the proletarian condition becomes generalized. Millions of small farmers and their farms, artisans, small shopkeepers with their independent enterprises, are wiped out. Their place taken, their status becomes that of "independent contractors," part-time employees of Walmart and other mass distribution outlets, etc. Whether in material or nonmaterial production, 90 percent of workers have, in one form or another, become waged employees. Earlier in this chapter I attempted to illustrate the consequences of diversity in the pay-scale, which, far from mapping directly the relative acquisition-cost of required skills, vastly exaggerates their disparity. Yet the sentiment of solidarity is being reborn. The Occupy movements take up the refrain "We are the 99 percent." Even though that 99 percent is really only 80 percent, it comprises a decisive majority of workers. This double reality—all are exploited by capital but in diverse forms and with differing degrees of violence—challenges the left. The left cannot afford, without giving up on a coherent program, to ignore "contradictions within the people," which, in turn, impose the need for diverse forms of organization and action by the new generalized proletariat. "Movement" ideology takes no notice of these challenges. But before it can return to the offensive, the left has the inescapable task of rebuilding central leaderships able to formulate its strategic objectives in coherent programmatic form.

On at least four levels the image of the generalized proletariat differs in the emergent and non-emergent peripheral countries in

1. whether the working class is becoming (as seen in the emerging countries) progressively stronger;
2. the persistence of a peasant class, whose members are nevertheless ever more integrated into the capitalist market and are thereby, albeit indirectly, subject to capitalist exploitation;
3. the dizzying growth of "survival" occupations resulting from lumpen-development;
4. the reactionary stance of major sectors of the middle classes, when they alone benefit from economic growth.

In the terminology of the Third International, the challenge here for the radical left is to "unite the workers and peasants"—to unite the working people, including those of the "informal" sectors, the critical intelligentsia, and the middle classes in a united front against the compradors.

The Novel Forms of Political Domination

Transformations of the system's economic foundations, with concomitant changes in class structure, have altered the modalities of political power. We have been brought to what I call the phase of "abstract capitalism," by which I mean that capitalism is no longer centered in bourgeois proprietary families—it is now expressed directly and exclusively through the power of money. That is why I consider Aglietta's term "proprietary capitalism" to be a misleading characterization of the regime. Financialization, which spreads the illusion that money "generates its own offspring" without any connection to actual production, expresses to the very highest degree contemporary capitalism's abstract character.

Political domination henceforward is exerted through a new-style "political class" and a media clergy, both entirely at the service of abstract generalized-monopoly capitalism. The new modalities by which capital exerts its power are confirmed, not challenged, by the "sovereign individual" ideology and by the illusion of a "movement" that might transform the world and even "change our lives"—without ever posing the question of how the workers and the people are to take power.

In the peripheral countries, we reach the point of extreme caricature when lumpen-development gives power to a state and class of corruptionist compradors. On the other hand, in the emergent countries social coalitions of a different sort hold real power, deriving their legitimacy from the economic success of their political practice. This gives rise to the illusion that emergence "within globalized capitalism and by capitalist methods" would allow them to catch up. In fact, the limited possibilities available within that framework, and the resulting political and social conflicts, open the way to various potentialities, from the best (toward socialism) to the worst (failure and restoration of a comprador regime).

The Media Clergy and the New Political Class

I have copied the title of this section from a statement I heard at the Mouvement Politique d'Émancipation Populaire (MPEP) conference in October 2011. I believe the theme conveyed by that statement deserves to be developed. It seems to me that there is an irrefutable parallel between our contemporary society and the situation that prevailed in France on the eve of 1789. At that time, decision-making authority resided with the landed aristocracy, nobility who stood by their king. Nowadays, this power rests with the financial "plutocracy" in positions of power in capitalist monopolies the world over. In the France of yesteryear, this power was the preserve of "nobles of the robe"—bourgeoisie dressed in aristocratic robes. Today, the power of capitalistic monopolies is in the hands of the "political class," made up of bona fide financiers (in the ordinary finance sense of the word), associated with politicians from the traditional right wing and those from the electoral left. As for the aristocratic/monarchical political power of the Old Regime in France, it was sustained by the clergy of the Catholic Church, whose role was to give the regime a semblance of legitimacy by developing an appropriate casuistic rhetoric. Today, the onus is on the media to play this role. And the casuistry that it develops to accomplish this task and give the dominant power a veneer of legitimacy is characteristic of traditional methods devised by the religious clergy. My purpose here is to analyze the role played by "media clergy" in contemporary society. The subject of the "nobility of the robe" whose role is played today by politicians could be treated in the same vein.

Does Media Power Exist?

A cursory look at global reality across historical time frames would reveal the coexistence of multiple power structures. For example, in our contemporary world, economic power exists side by side with political power structures—legislative, executive, judiciary—exercised through established institutions that may be democratic or undemocratic. An example would be the power that ideological schools of thought and beliefs, religious and others, wield over people. Another example would be the power of the media that disseminate information, select, and make commentary about it. Recognizing this plurality is an extremely banal task. The real question that begs to be asked is the following: How do these powers, diverse as they are, get organized to complement each other in the functions they fulfill in the construction of the social fabric, or otherwise enter into confrontation in the field? Undoubtedly, the response to this question can only be concrete; in other words, it deals with specific societies at specific historical periods. The reflections that follow focus on the articulation of relations between media powers and facets of social power structures in contemporary capitalist societies.

One more word on the notion of media power: abundant literature is out there that analyzes the diverse qualifications of human beings, including their *homo communicans* character. The implication of this is that the volume and intensity of information to which human beings have access, without taking into account what they were in the past, would have really transformed human beings and society. This may be an exaggeration, given that from the outset, human beings have always identified with the power of speech, means of communication par excellence. It ensues from this affirmation that the proposition regarding the volume and intensity of information is by its own definition correct and by this token endows the media, which is the essence of its existence, some power, as well as increasing moral, political, and social responsibilities. However, this observation does not preclude the pertinence of the following question: How does this media power relate to others?

Media Power in the Contemporary Capitalist System: Myths and Realities

Media power, like all power structures, is not—has never been, and cannot be, "independent." I am not implying that media power is under the aegis of another power structure (political, religious, or economic). No, media power can be, and actually is, generally autonomous. What I mean to say is that in its functions it enjoys an autonomy that is inherent to it, distinct from the reproductive logic of other power structures. This autonomy is analogous with the autonomy enjoyed by the Catholic clergy in France under the ancien régime. The clergy in France functioned like other religious clergies of the time. This is the role the new media clergy play today.

Media autonomy translates into ethical deontology. In this perspective, there are media outlets that are at the beck and call of others; there are some that are not. This notwithstanding, this autonomy. which is a democratic ideal for its practitioners, is not synonymous with the notion of media independence, which is an absolute concept, whereas the concept of autonomy implies articulation (interdependence) among different powers, including the media. Thus the whole notion of articulation remains central and unavoidable. Now, I maintain that in the contemporary capitalist system (the one in which we have lived for about forty years), a superior power appears to have imposed itself on the rest. It subordinates all these other powers and makes them comply with its dictates. I am referring to a strong trend and not a state of fait accompli. This is because resistance to the articulation of this tendency is strong, and perhaps becomes reenforced over time. The supreme power to which I am making reference here is that of "globalized financial monopolies."

In brief, we are dealing here with economic power, and this power is the product of the evolution that results in the extreme centralization of prosperity and management of capital, with no similarity to what it was only half a century ago. These monopolies (or oligopolies if you prefer to use this term) directly or indirectly control the entirety of the productive systems (and this is new), not only at the level of dominant traditional capitalist ventures—the most developed countries brought together under the umbrella of the Triad of United States/ Europe/Japan—but also at the global level. Certainly, this tendency is taking concrete shape through economic and political action strategies—and has to face resistance from emerging economies like China and others. This qualitative transformation has reduced the relative space of autonomy that political power traditionally benefited from within the Triad under consideration—an autonomy that gave meaning and significance to "bourgeois democracy," worldview, current trends, "consensus" on religious beliefs, in short, "trends of the time." To put this differently, what is unfolding is not what is called a "market economy" but a "market-oriented society." Within this framework, media, as well as political organizations, realize that their autonomy has diminished, relatively speaking. Without necessarily becoming instruments at the beck and call of others, they find themselves in situations where they have to fulfill useful functions that are necessary to guarantee the success of deployments of supreme powers of global monopolies.

Thus we are not living in an era of advanced democracy; on the contrary, we are witnessing the disfigurement and retrogression of democratic values. A citizen who tries to understand the true state of affairs is subjected to tribulations that make him feel depoliticized. But there is no democracy without politically savvy citizens who are capable of thinking creatively and conceiving alternative ways of doing things coherently and differently. In lieu of these kinds of individuals, one finds passive people, devoid of authentic freedom, reduced to the status of passive consumers/spectators. These individuals are often asked to endorse a consensus, a false consensus that is nothing but a reflection of the sacrosanct demands of the executives in global monopolies. In this scenario, elections are transformed into a farce, in which "candidates" whose managerial modus operandi in the organization of power structures shows signs of the existence of para-personnel aligned behind the same consensus. The apogee of this farce is reached when "ratings agencies" (in other words, employees of these monopolies) identify the limits of feasibility.

Now, sadly enough, major media networks are part and parcel of the distillation of this unilateral thought pattern, the very opposite of critical thinking. Certainly, the media does not always resort to falsehood. Respectable media outlets try to steer clear of easily discovered malpractices. But they do pick and choose, and their commentaries constitute the messages their owners expect from them. Therefore, their autonomy is reduced to the institutionalization of a functional casuistry that gives legitimacy to the powers that be. It is in this sense that I contend that the power of financial aristocracy is complemented by the power of media clergy. One could provide countless examples of instances of the media casuistry that hails criminal judges as champions of democracy (like the judge in Libya who passed a death sentence on Bulgarian nurses), and presents Arabs such as the Sultan of Qatar and the King of Saudi Arabia as advocates of democracy. It is hard to imagine a more effective fraud than this one.

An example of casuistry by media clergy is the question of intervention (military, humanitarian, economic, etc.) by imperialists in the affairs of the South. It is forbidden to open a debate on the real motives behind these interventions, notably in matters relating to access to the natural resources of the countries in question, or the establishment of military bases there. It should be noted that the reasons for these interventions are often only those given by Western powers. As far as democratic precepts are concerned, these powers expect southerners to take their word at face value. "Democrats" do not tell lies. They make you believe or make believe that these interventions have been agreed upon by the international community. It is forbidden to remind people that this international community is represented by no one but the ambassador of the United States as well as ambassadors from small allies from the European Union/NATO, at times supported by a few countries like Qatar. It is necessary to believe or make believe that the real motives behind these interventions are presented to us by intervening forces: liberate a people caught in the lair of a bloody dictatorship, promote democracy, and come to the aid of victims of repression. From the outset, the media assumes the posture of "analyst" (in fact, phony analysts of reality). The role of the public, then, is to observe whether or not the intended objectives have been achieved; whether serious blunders have been committed; and whether unforeseen obstacles have stymied the accomplishment of set goals. There is great casuistry that prevents role-players from taking the debate to the field: what the real motives behind these interventions are.

Need for Media that Work to Re-Politicize Citizens

During the French Revolution, some members of the "lower clergy" dissociated themselves from the hierarchy of the aristocracy to contribute to the formation of a new citizenry endowed with the capacity to engage in real critical thinking. A similar process is noticeable in the media today. There is no question that proponents of media's new deal, which would be truly democratic, are up against stiff competition from the "big media" that has access to huge financial resources. One can only salute and support the contributions made by this minority.

An honorable media power conceives its responsibility as analogous to that of independent and politically conscious citizens who have the wherewithal to contribute to the construction of what I have code-named, with peers in the Forum Mondial des Alternatives, the convergence of struggles with respect for diversity. The point here is not to subscribe to a single school of thought—which strives to provide legitimacy for the practices of global monopolies—but another singular thought pattern. It is not an appeal to juxtapose ideas and projects that are considered equally legitimate. The point is to engage in patient and sustained work in a bid to contribute to the development of critical thought that is likely to give direction to social and political struggles geared toward the emancipation of spirits and human beings, individually and collectively, in their common struggle. The notion of diversity as used here is not restricted to the choice of specific battlefields. Our conceptualization of diversity harbors the idea of appreciating instruments of social theory conceived to deepen the analytical thought pattern on the real world. It also takes into account the meaning provided by all and sundry on the perception of desired emancipation. Then and only then would the media acquire power that could be wielded responsibly in order to give recognition to the quest and definition of immediate objectives in the struggle and in long-term perspectives to which the media wants to subscribe.

The New Political Class

During the extended nineteenth century, until the emergence of generalized monopoly capitalism (the years 1975–1990), bourgeois democracy was real. Its reality derived from the fact that it expressed historical compromises linking the capitalist bourgeoisie sometimes with the former aristocracies, sometimes with the peasantry, later with the working class (in the post–Second World War welfare states). Competing political parties represented the various interests within the dominant coalition. Politicians (few women among them, at the time) were socially, and often territorially, based. The same held true of the parties and organizations (trade union, among others) outside the dominant coalitions.

Such is no longer the case. Politics has become a trade, that of power brokers for the generalized monopolies. Political parties are no longer straightforward representatives of differing interests within society. They have become action groups, specialists in shaping a "consensus" public opinion. They merely each devise their own rhetorical tricks, distinctive but ultimately complementary, for appealing to particular "sensibilities." This search for consensus deprives the "right–left" dichotomy of all meaning.

Senile Capitalism and the End of Bourgeois Civilization

The characteristics of the new ruling classes are no mere passing phenomena. They correspond strictly to what is required for the operations of contemporary capitalism.

Bourgeois civilization—like every civilization—amounts to more than the mechanisms for reproduction of its economic system. It used to feature a moral and ideological element, with praise for individual initiative, but also for honesty and respect for law, and even for social solidarity at least as expressed on the national level. This value system, stamped on the milieu of political personnel at its service, guaranteed a certain stability to the overall reproduction of its social system. This value system is disappearing, to be replaced by a valueless system. Evidence is seen all over for this transformation: criminal U.S. presidents, buffoons like Berlusconi at the head of European states, run-of-the-mill autocrats in so many countries of the South, whose despotism has nothing at all enlightened about it, obscurantists on the make, all of them unreserved admirers of the "American model." "Uncultured" and "vulgar" are appropriate terms for a growing majority in that "society of rulers." So dramatic an evolution foretells the end of a civilization. It is a replay of what history displayed in its decadent epochs. A "new world" is indeed being made. But not the better world wished for, so naïvely, by many social movements that, aware of the damages, are blind to their causes. A world much worse than that came to prevail.

For all these reasons, I maintain that contemporary oligopolistic capitalism must henceforward be considered senile, despite any seeming short-term successes it might enjoy. Its rulers succeed only in advancing a new barbarism, which I delineated thirty years ago in my essay "Revolution or Decadence."

Generalized-Monopoly Capitalism in Crisis

The system commonly termed "neoliberalism," which in fact is the system of financialized, globalized, and generalized monopoly capitalism, is imploding before our eyes. This system, plainly unable to overcome its growing internal contradictions, cannot avoid plunging forward in its mad race.

The "crisis" of the system is due to nothing other than its own "success." To this very day the strategy implemented by the monopolies has consistently produced its intended effects: "austerity" plans are still in effect despite all resistance. To this very day the initiative remains in the hands of the monopolies—"the markets"—and their political servants the governments, whose decisions are determined in submission to the demands of the markets. The system of generalized monopolies has entered on a crisis proving its incapacity for stable development. We are dealing with a crisis of capitalist civilization that places on the agenda of what is necessary and possible the construction of a higher stage of civilization—which is to say, entrance onto the long transition to socialism.

To analyze the struggles and conflicts now under way, to see their perspectives as calling into question imperialist domination itself, will allow us to place correctly a new phenomenon: the emergence of some countries of the South.

REFERENCES

Some of the issues raised in this chapter have been developed in several of my own works :

Délégitimer le capitalisme (Brussels: Contradictions, 2011), especially the chapters "Surplus and Imperialist Rent," 11–16, 39–40) and "Abstract Labor," 95–103.
From Capitalism to Civilisation (Delhi: Tulika Books, 2010), which deals in part with the productivity of social labor.
The Liberal Virus (London: Pluto, 2004), which examines ideological issues.
Ending the Crisis of Capitalism or Ending Capitalism (Oxford: Pambazuka, 2010), covering generalized monopolies.
"Surplus in Monopoly Capital and Imperialist Rent," *Monthly Review* 64/3 (July–August 2012).

See also:

Anton Pannekoek and Patrick Tort, *Darwinisme et marxisme* (Paris: Arkhé, 2011).
Wang Hui, *The End of the Revolution* (London: Verso, 2012).
Jean Claude Delaunay, "La Chine, la France, la France, la Chine," Fondation Gabriel Péri, 2012. Available at www.gabrielperi.fr/La-Chine-la-France-la-France-la?lang=fr.

2. THE SOUTH: EMERGING COUNTRIES AND LUMPEN-DEVELOPMENT

WHAT IS "EMERGING"? This term has been used by some to mean one thing and by others something entirely different in different contexts, often without any caution regarding precision. I will therefore define the sense that I will give to the set of economic, social, political, and cultural transformations that permit one to speak of the "emergence" of a state, a nation, and a people who have been placed in a peripheral place in the capitalist world system.

Emergence is not measured by a rising rate of GDP growth or exports over a long period of time (more than a decade), nor by the fact that the society in question has obtained a higher level of GDP per capita, as defined by the World Bank, aid institutions controlled by Western powers, and conventional economists. Emergence involves much more: a sustained growth in industrial production in a state and a strengthening of the capacity of these industries to be competitive on a global scale. Again, one must define which specific industries are important and what is meant by competitiveness.

Extractive industries (minerals and fossil fuels) must be excluded from this definition. In states endowed by nature with these resources, accelerated growth can occur without necessarily leaving in its wake productive activities. The extreme example of this situation of "non-emergence" would be the Gulf States, Venezuela, Gabon, and others.

One must also understand that the competitiveness of productive activities in the economy should be considered as a productive system in its entirety and not a certain unit of production alone. Due to the preference for outsourcing and subcontracting, multinationals operating in the South can be the impetus for the creation of local units of production tied to transnationals, or autonomous and capable of exporting to the world market, which earns them the status of "competitive" in the language of conventional economists. This truncated concept of competitiveness, which proceeds from an empiricist method, is not ours. Competitiveness is that of a productive system. For this to exist, the economy must be made up of productive elements, with branches of this production sufficiently interdependent that one can speak of it as a system.

Competitiveness depends upon diverse economic and social factors, among others the general level of education and training of workers on all levels and the efficiency of the group of institutions that manage the national political economy—fiscal policy, business law, labor law, credit, social services, etc. The productive system cannot reduce productive transformation only to activities involved in manufacturing and consumption—although the absence of these annuls the existence of a productive system worthy of the name—rather it must integrate food and agriculture as services required for the normal functioning of the system.

A real productive system can be more or less "advanced." By this I mean that the group of activities must be qualified: is it involved in "banal" productions or high technologies? It is important to situate an emerging state using this point of view: in what measure is it on the path of generating value-added products?

The question of emergence therefore requires both a political and holistic examination. A state cannot be emerging if it is not inward, rather than outward, looking with the goal of creating a domestic market and thus reasserting national economic sovereignty. This complex objective requires sovereignty over all aspects of economic life. In particular, it demands policies that protect food security and sovereignty, and equally sovereignty over one's natural resources and access to others outside of one's territory. These multiple and complementary objectives are contrasted with those of the comprador class, who are content to adopt growth models that meet the requirements of the dominant global system (liberal internationalism) and the possibilities these offer.

This proposed definition of emergence does not address the question of the political strategy of the state and society: capitalism or socialism? However this question cannot be left out of the debate, as the choice made by the leading classes will have major effects, both positive and negative, for a successful emergence. I would not say that the only option is to follow a capitalist perspective, which implements a system of a capitalist nature—control and exploitation of the workforce and a free market. Nor would I suggest that only a radical socialist option that challenges these forms of capitalism—property, organized labor, market controls—is able to last over long periods of time and move the society forward in the world system.

The links between the politics of emergence on one hand and the accompanying social transformation on the other do not depend solely on the internal coherence of the former, but equally its degree of complementarity, or conflict, with the latter. Social struggles, whether class-based or political, do not adjust themselves to fit the logic of a state's implementation of an emergence. Rather they are a determinant of this program. Current experience shows the diversity and dynamism of these links. Emergence is often accompanied by inequalities. One must examine the nature of these: inequalities where the beneficiaries are a tiny minority or a large minority (the middle class) and are realized in a framework that promotes the pauperization of the majority of workers, or, on the contrary, one where the same people see a betterment in their quality of life, even if the growth rates of compensation for workers will be less than those who benefit from the system. Said in another manner, politics can associate emergence with pauperization or not. Emergence does not follow a definitive set of rules. Rather, it is a series of successive steps; the first can prepare the way for following successes or bring about deadlock.

In the same manner the relation between the emerging economy and the global economy is constantly transforming as well. From these two different perspectives come policies that can promote sovereignty or weaken it, and at the same time promote social solidarity in the nation or weaken it. Emergence is therefore not synonymous with growth in exports and an increase in power measured in such a manner. Growth in exports can strengthen or weaken the autonomy of an emerging state relative to the world market.

We cannot speak of emergence in general, nor can we speak of models—Chinese, Indian, Brazilian, and Korean—in general. One must concretely examine, in each case, the successive steps in the evolution of their emergence, identify the strong and weak points, and analyze the dynamic of their implementation and the associated contradictions.

Emergence is a political as well as an economic project. The measure of success is therefore determined by reducing the means by which the countries in the dominant capitalist center perpetuate their domination, despite the fact that economic success of emergent states is measured in conventional economic terms. I define the means as control of the dominant powers over the areas of technological development, access to natural resources, the global financial system, dissemination of information, and weapons of mass destruction. The imperialist collective Triad—United States, Europe, and Japan—intends to conserve, using all of these means, their privileged positions in dominating the planet and prohibiting emergent states from bringing this domination into question. I conclude that the ambitions of emergent states enter into conflict with the strategic objectives of the Triad, and the measure of the violence emanating from this conflict will be determined by the degree of radicalism with which the emergent state challenges the aforementioned privileges of the center.

Economic emergence is not separable from the foreign policies of the states. Do they align themselves with the military and political coalition of the Triad? Do they accept strategies put in place by NATO? Conversely, will they oppose them?

Emergence and Lumpen-Development

There can be no emergence without state politics resting on a comfortable social bloc, a social force that gives it legitimacy and the capabability of constructing a coherent project, an inward-looking national productive system. This must at the same time ensure the participation of the great majority of social classes and see to it that these social classes receive the benefits of growth.

Opposing the favorable evolution of an authentic emergence is the fact that there is typically a unilateral submission to the requirements of the implementation of global capitalism and general monopolies, which produce nothing other than what I call lumpen-development. I will now liberally borrow from the late André Gunder Frank, who analyzed a similar evolution, albeit at a different time and place. Today lumpen-development is the product of accelerated social disintegration associated with the "development" model (which does not deserve its name) imposed by the monopolies of the imperialist core on the peripheral societies they dominate. It is manifested by a dizzying growth of subsistence activities, called the informal sphere—otherwise called the pauperization associated with the unilateral logic of accumulation of capital.

One can remark that I did not qualify the emergence as "capitalist" or "socialist." This is because emergence is a process associated with complementarity, and at the same time conflict in the logic of capitalist management of the economy and the logics of "non-capitalist"—and potentially socialist—management of society and politics.

Among the experiences of emergence, some cases merit special mention as they are not associated with the processes of lumpen-development. There is no pauperization among the popular classes, but rather progress in the living standards, modest or otherwise. Two of these experiences are clearly capitalist, those of South Korea and Taiwan (I will not discuss here the particular historical conditions that permitted the success of the implementation in the two countries). Two others inherited the aspirations conducted in the name of socialism—Vietnam and China. Cuba could also be included in this group if it can master the contradictions through which it is currently going.

But we know of other cases of emergence that have been associated with lumpen-development of a massive nature. India is the best example. There are segments of this project that correspond to the requirements of emergence. There is a state policy that favors the building of an industrial productive system. Consequently, there is an associated expansion of the middle classes and progress in technological capacities and education. These are capable of playing autonomously on the chessboard of international politics. But for a grand majority, two-thirds of society, there is accelerated pauperization. We have therefore a hybrid system that ties together emergence and lumpen-development. We can highlight the link between these two complementary parts of reality. Without suggesting too gross a generalization, all the other cases considered emergent belong to this familiar hybrid, which includes Brazil, South Africa, and others.

But there exist also, and it is most of the other southern countries, situations in which there are no elements of emergence because the processes of lumpen-development occupy much of the society. The three countries considered below—Turkey, Iran, Egypt—are part of this group, and it is for this reason that I declare them non-emergent and the projects of emergence abandoned.

Failed Emergence: Turkey, Iran, and Egypt

The reflections that follow concern the failure of Turkish, Iranian, and Egyptian attempts at emergence, long ago and in the recent past, their frustration due to the intervention of imperialist powers or by the lack of capacity to challenge them, and the notions of today's leading classes, which render doubtful the prospect of any of these three countries emerging. The reflections must be understood in the context of the theoretical framework of the preceding pages.

These three Middle Eastern states should normally have been found in lists of today's "emerging" states. They have each attempted, in the past, to modernize as a response to the challenge from Europe. Egypt attempted this under Pacha Mohamed Ali in the nineteenth century, as well as under Nasser in the twentieth. In Ottoman Turkey, the Tanzimat, a reorganization aimed at modernizing the state, and later endeavors during the time of Atatürk (1920–45), can be seen as the same. Iran began with its revolution in 1907, and later, the reign of Reza Pahlavi (until 1979). These states were, in their own manner, leaders in modernizing transformation of capitalist peripheries in the nineteenth and twentieth centuries. However, today none of these three states could reasonably be called "emerging," not in the same way as China, South Korea, South Africa, Brazil, Argentina, and others. The three states of focus are all important, in their own right, and also have similar populations of around 80 million people.

Turkey

Is Turkey European? The debates around this question are extremely polemical and lack a solid scientific foundation. It is important to note that the ruling classes have considered themselves so for a long time, going back to the Ottoman Age and 1453 when Mehmet El Fateh, the conqueror of Constantinople, hesitated, reflected, and decided not to proclaim himself "Emperor of Byzantium/Constantinople," as the soldiers, who had battled under the banner of Islam as ghazis or conquerors, would not have accepted it. Still, in the nineteenth century, Ottoman Turkey engaged in a reorganization of the state known as Tanzimat—"reorganization" or "perestroika"—the purpose of which can be clearly seen: to make Turkey a "European" state. Whether the Ottoman/Turkish society advanced in this direction, or if the progress remained insignificant, is a question of which there has been no shortage of examination by historians.

Toward the end of the nineteenth century, a large number of intellectuals and Ottoman politicians, Turkish or otherwise, organized themselves under the name "Young Turks" to accelerate this pace, beginning by ridding themselves of a Sultan judged incapable of imagining either the overthrow of his empire or the abandonment of its imperial character (the control of Arab Mashriq). Echoing European nationalist ideologies, they identified themselves overtly as Turks rather than Ottomans. The war of 1914–18 created the conditions to unambiguously implement the Young Turks' program, under the leadership of Mustafa Kemal (Atatürk). The Arab provinces were lost, the caliphate was abolished, and the war against the intervention of the Entente was won. The newly proclaimed Turkish Republic could imagine itself on the route toward successful Europeanization.

It was unquestionably a project of emergence. It was also carried out by a capitalist transformation of society. All that was necessary, they believed, was the desire for power. The idea that the logic of global capitalism, with its creation of a global system consisting of a polarization between the core and integrated partners in the periphery, would not permit this development was unthinkable at that time. The fact that Atatürk's project coincided with the Russian Revolution could have raised questions regarding the appropriateness of a capitalist approach. But Atatürk and his contemporaries did not dwell on this thought, and the Turkish Communists had even fewer clear ideas on the question. Social reality was to shape the implementation of the new attempt at emergence. A capitalist "bourgeoisie" was, at most, in its infancy in 1924 Turkey. However, there was an important class of intellectuals, politicians, and bureaucrats—only male—and the military who were responsible for assuming the leadership of the country. This class was recruited from the western part of the country—Istanbul, Edirne, Smyrna—and was identified, by themselves and others, as "Rumelian," from the original Rome, or Byzantium, which indicated cultural aspirations. The east, Anatolia, was made up exclusively of peasants. The Turks at that time recognized Rumelians as "civilized" or "European" and Anatolians as wretches in need of being civilized. Of course, the Rumelians were generally secular or even atheist, while the Anatolians were devoutly Muslim.

The Rumelians and followers of Atatürk were nationalist in the intolerant and chauvinistic manner of the term. They would never recognize the Armenian genocide, and the shameful treatment to which the rarely spared Armenian child was subjected (forced conversion to Islam and discrimination) nor the situation of the Kurds or the Arabs of Hatay. All of the governments in Ankara, even the Islamists of today, share this chauvinism. The "Arab" ideologues of political Islam privilege the Islamic identity to the point where other identities are nearly forgotten. We are neither Algerians, Arabs, nor Berbers, but Muslims, proclaim these ideologues. Political Islam in Turkey shares this somewhat but not fully; a Turk is Muslim, but just as much Turk.

The only development model possible in this situation would be state capitalism led by an enlightened despot. The implementation of the model would benefit the popular masses, both urban and rural, by allowing them to climb in the social hierarchy through children's education, as well as receive a higher quality of life. The benefits of enlightened despotism brought about an incontestable legitimacy in the eyes of the people. It did not hurt that it was also linked with anti-imperial struggles. This is precisely where the attempt at emergence diverges from the Arab states. The nationalist powers of the latter, as we will see from the example of Nasser's Egypt, were systematically attacked by the imperialist powers. The Turkish regime never was. This was both its strength and its weakness.

From 1945, Turkey, still Kemalist, opted for a Western alliance against the Soviet threat (determined unfortunately by Stalin's claims that year concerning Kars and Ardahan and the status of the Bosphorus Strait). Turkey would become a founding member of NATO, at a time when no requirement existed that the members make any declaration of democracy. The weakness of the Kemalist capitalist state permitted it, as an American ally instead of opponent, to integrate into the global capitalist system that followed the war. Washington "counseled" Ankara and secured "elections" in 1950 that brought Menderes to power. But his electoral victory would transform the relations between the Kemalist/Rumelian forces and the Anatolian peasantry. Menderes looked toward a class of newly rich Anatolian peasants, produced by agricultural development. The end of the Rumelian/Kemalist elite's privilege had begun and would only continue. The new model, suggested and supported by the United States, the World Bank, and their contemporaries, effectively emphasized the development of capitalist agriculture. But the rich peasants remained "Muslim," in opposition to the Kemalist state. The compradorization of the Turkish development path occurred gradually yet plainly: capitalist agriculture, openness toward industrial outsourcing, privatization of large parts of the originally capitalist state, possibilities for mass emigration of the poor Anatolian peasantry. The new class of businessmen associated with and benefiting from the compradorian development was recruited primarily from the children of the rich Anatolian peasantry.

Politically, the last defenders of Kemalism, the army, would travel from defeat to defeat, despite the restoration of the dictatorship twice, until the day, only some years distant, when Anatolian Turkish political Islam would be established as henceforth dominant in society. This evolution, which I define as a re-compradorization, which ends the Kemalist project of emergence, is accompanied by the strong affirmation of the continued importance of the essential tenet of NATO, that being the support for the strategies of the imperialist Triad. It is in this sense that I say that Turkey was "the Colombia of the Middle East." For those who question this affirmation, I direct their attention to the recent interventions of Ankara in the ongoing Syrian crisis.

It should be understood that the Americans' Turkish ally remains a candidate for accession to the European Union (EU). However, there is no contradiction, but rather a complementarity, between membership in this Union and NATO. This project of "Europeanization," which nourishes the illusion that the new Turkey has inherited the mantle of Kemalism, constitutes a real, albeit minor, question. That different European political forces in the EU accept while others reject Turkey's candidacy and that the justification of these postures ends in polemics (never a "Muslim" country in "Christian" Europe) constitute equally real questions, but again of lesser importance. But compradorization, the antithesis of emergence, is completed by the enthusiasm of its cheerleaders for the EU. So will Turkey rediscover the Middle East? Or perhaps even Turan? How would this eventually happen?

Turkey is active in the Middle East. But what role does it fill? In fact, Turkey intervenes as an ally of the United States and not as an autonomous emerging power. This is not new. Turkey was at the center of the Baghdad Pact rejected by Nasser following the 1958 Iraq Revolution. Turkey is, and remains, the military ally of Israel. It presently intervenes in Syria at the behest of Washington. Turkey is therefore easily "the Colombia of the Middle East." The Turanian alternative to reject Europeanization was tried first in 1918 by Enver Pacha. But the rise of the Soviet Union rendered these ambitions impossible, although after its collapse it appeared that it could be reborn from the ashes. However, Turkey can hardly do more than be a subordinate ally implementing the plan of its American masters.

Postures taken by the powers in the South are not neutral in the effects on the orientation of economic development. Inclusion in the geostrategic considerations of the imperialist powers is naturally associated with economic compradorization, the antithesis of emergence. Turkish political Islam is, like the Arab states or Pakistan, reactionary in its social postures; it overtly opposes the struggles of workers and peasants. This is in line with what is permitted in the corridors of power in the West, whose leaders are always therefore eager to certify their democracy.

Emergent states must enter into conflict with the dominant imperialists, even if the intensity of the conflict is variable from moment to moment. How prepared are they, though, to be treated as an adversary by the imperialist powers in order to be a candidate for emergence?

Iran

Iran is an old and great nation, proud of its history, which reacted strongly, and quite early, to the European menace, both English and Russian. From 1907, its people began a revolution against the regime of the decadent Qadjars dynasty, which was judged incapable of resisting foreigners. Moreover, many intellectuals who participated in the revolution were trained in the Russian Caucasus with the Russian Social Democratic Labor Party, which would later produce Bolshevism. This left many leading Iranians with a much firmer grasp than elsewhere of certain issues and of the relation between imperialist domination and the historical pattern of exploitative class relations (feudal system).

The new power of Pahlavi, established in 1921, addressed this fact in a particular manner: this monarchy was reactionary to the overtures for social change—but refused to be the lackeys for the dominant forces of the world market. The long-term effects of the Soviet presence in the north of the country during the Second World War, the support given to the construction of the autonomous Azerbaijan and Kurdish societies and states, the emergence of a powerful anti-imperialist and socialist party (the Toudeh), and the nationalist position taken in 1951 by the prime minister, Mossadeqh, who nationalized oil, could not be erased by the CIA-sponsored coup that permitted Mohamed Reza Shah to turn the tide and rejoin the Western camp.

To defend against the challenge of the powerful democratic, nationalist, and progressive forces in Iran, Mohamed Reza Shah engaged in a "White Revolution," beginning in 1962, which was associated with a "neutral" international posture. Land reform was not really part of this; it did not reduce the power and the riches of the latifundia; even though modernization was encouraged, this merely facilitated the rise of a newly rich peasant class. Added to this was the modernization of morals (especially toward women) and an effort in the domain of education. The neutral postures—reconciliation with the USSR in 1965, China in 1970, another nationalization of oil in 1973—were, in these conditions, accepted by the Western powers, which had no better alternative. The regime, heavily dependent on security (the crimes of their political police, the Savak, have gained a well-earned notoriety) were the only way to maintain a reactionary social order. The emergence project of Mohamed Reza Shah was certainly one conceived in the manner of capitalism, albeit a state capitalism. The limits and contradictions were products of having chosen this option and principle.

The destruction of Toudeh by police violence cleared the path for a new force to challenge the regime. This was organized around Shiite Mullahs and their leader, the Ayatollah Khomeini. The Islamist regime, in place since 1979, is also undermined by its internal contradictions. At its foundation, in regard to its desires to reconstruct society, it is reactionary, not only in its cultural approaches (women are veiled) but also in its relations to economic and social life. Most of its support is provided by two social groups: the Bazaris, or the commercial/comprador traditional bourgeoisie, and the newly rich peasants. The regime inherited a state capitalism managed by "technocrats" allied to the Shah's dictatorship. What the regime did was simply substitute this "civil" management with a religious one. The Mullahs in managerial positions enriched themselves with no regard for the overall coherence of the Shah's modernization project, which became modernization led by religious figures, equally troubled by its own limits and contradictions. However, as the Shah's regime had been pro-Western, the new regime could adorn itself with an anti-imperialist mantle, although this posture would be confused with anti-Western.

The confusion is extreme. It explains how many Western analysts can qualify the system as "modernizing" ("modern Islam," they say). They base this on real evolutions, but mistake the significance that these are given. Of course, the female marriage age has been raised, and a larger number of women are working as well as occupying the same roles and responsibilities. But this progress is found throughout the South (with the exception of the Gulf States) as in the North (where the word *change* is well understood). Modernity, not to mention emancipation, requires much more.

Washington had supported the Shah until the end, and its reaction elicited the expected nationalist Iranian stance. This is why Washington mobilized its erstwhile ally, Iraq's Saddam Hussein, to engage in ten years of criminal and irrational war beginning in 1980. This led to a constitution, under the aegis of Washington, of an Arab camp (the Gulf-supporting Iraq) who initiated the Iran (Shiite)–Gulf (Sunni for the most part) hostility. This conflict has been described as atavistic. There exists, however, no supporting facts of this conflict as a return to one that has permeated the region through history, as if there were an imminent, constant and invariable reality. With the assistance of falsehoods, it could appear to be so: reactionary political Islam allied with one or another group. In this manner Iran (Islamic, Shiite, Khomeiniist) became the adversary of the Western powers, even if they had not wanted it to. Iran under Khomeini could not conceive of managing the economy other than by the simple rules of capitalism. A modus vivendi would have been easy to find between this local capitalism and that on the global scale. The Mullahs, particularly those who advance "reforms," have studied such a path. The Gulf sought to frustrate these attempts, by alarming Washington.

Tehran's nuclear option can do nothing but further poison the atmosphere. This is not a new initiative of the Khomeini regime. Rather, it was the Shah Mohamed Reza who started his country down this path. During his time, Washington had nothing to say. Khomeini's regime did nothing but continue along the same route. There is no reason to reproach them, even using the hypothesis that behind the civil nuclear program lies a nuclear weapons program. They have truly no reason to accept the point of view of Washington, and its subordinate allies in NATO, concerning proliferation. One is not declared dangerous or a potential adversary unless the declaration benefits the imperialist powers. The silence concerning Israel's monstrous nuclear equipment shows the Western powers' method of judgment: differing weights, differing measures. Were denuclearization to occur (the best possible option), it could be initiated only by the most menacing state in the world, the United States. One concludes, therefore, that the threat of aggression against Iran proceeds directly from those howling in Tel Aviv.

The situation is also more complex because the occupation of Iraq and the standoff in Afghanistan have not given Washington the results it desires. Certainly Iraq has been destroyed, not only the state (split into four de facto regimes: Sunni, Shiite, Kurd 1, and Kurd 2) but the society as well. Among other things, all scientists were assassinated under the orders of the occupier. But the destruction of Iraq has at the same time given Iran a formidable card to play; it can mobilize its (Shiite) allies if needed. To combat this problem, Washington has decided to weaken Iran by destroying its regional allies, beginning with Syria.

All of this confirms that the political conflict between the United States and Iran is very real. But that does not change the question posed in this reflection: Is Iran on the path to emergence? My pure and simple response is no. Nothing in the evolution of Iran's economic system permits one to see the state leave the lumpen-development in which Khomeini's state is stuck. It is not enough to be considered an adversary by the imperialist powers to become, miraculously, an emergent state.

Egypt

Egypt was the first country in the periphery of globalized capitalism that tried to "emerge." Even at the start of the nineteenth century, well before Japan and China, the Viceroy Mohammed Ali had conceived and undertaken a program of renovation for Egypt and its near neighbors in the Arab Mashreq (Mashreq means "east," that is, eastern North Africa and the Levant). That vigorous experiment took up two-thirds of the nineteenth century and only belatedly ran out of breath in the 1870s, during the second half of the reign of the Khedive Ismail. The analysis of its failure cannot ignore the violence of the foreign aggression by Great Britain, the foremost power of industrial capitalism during that period. Twice, in the naval campaign of 1840 and then by taking control of the Khedive's finances during the 1870s, and then finally by military occupation in 1882, England fiercely pursued its objective: to make sure that a modern Egypt would fail to emerge. Certainly the Egyptian project was subject to the limitations of its time since it manifestly envisaged emergence within and through capitalism, unlike Egypt's second attempt at emergence, which we will discuss further on. That project's own social contradictions, like its underlying political, cultural, and ideological presuppositions, were undoubtedly responsible, at least in part, for its failure. The fact remains that without imperialist aggression, those contradictions would probably have been overcome, as they were in Japan. Beaten, emergent Egypt was forced to undergo nearly forty years (1880–1920) as a servile periphery, whose institutions were refashioned in service to that period's model of capitalist/imperialist accumulation. That imposed retrogression struck not only its productive system, but also the country's political and social institutions. Egypt operated systematically to reinforce all the reactionary and medieval cultural and ideological conceptions that had been useful for keeping the country in its subordinate position.

The Egyptian nation—its people, its elites—never accepted that position. This stubborn refusal in turn gave rise to a second wave of rising movements, which unfolded during the next half-century (1919–67). Indeed, I see that period as a continuous series of struggles and major forward movements. It had a triple objective: democracy, national independence, and social progress. These three objectives—however limited and sometimes confused their formulations—were inseparable one from the other. In this reading, the chapter of Nasserist systematization (1955–67) is nothing but the final chapter of that long series of advancing struggles, which began with the revolution of 1919–20.

The first moment of that half-century of rising emancipation struggles in Egypt had put its emphasis—with the formation of the Wafd in 1919—on political modernization through adoption in 1923 of a bourgeois form of constitutional democracy (limited monarchy) and on the reconquest of independence. The form of democracy envisaged allowed progressive secularization—if not secularism in the radical sense of that term—whose symbol was the flag linking cross and crescent (a flag that reappeared in the demonstrations of January and February 2011). "Normal" elections were then allowed, without the least problem, not merely for Copts (native Egyptian Christians) to be elected by Muslim majorities but for those very Copts to hold high positions in the state. The British put their full power, supported actively by a reactionary bloc composed of the monarchy, the great landlords, and the rich peasants, into undoing the democratic progress made by Egypt under Wafdist leadership. In the 1930s the dictatorship of Sedki Pasha, abolishing the democratic 1923 constitution, clashed with the student movement then spearheading the democratic anti-imperialist struggles. It was not by chance that, to counter this threat, the British Embassy and the Royal Palace actively supported the formation in 1927 of the Muslim Brotherhood, inspired by "Islamist" thought in its most backward "salafist" version of Wahhabism as formulated by Rachid Reda. This was the most reactionary version, anti-democratic and against social progress, of the newborn "political Islam." The conquest of Ethiopia undertaken by Mussolini, with world war looming, forced London to make some concessions to the democratic forces. In 1936, the Wafd, having learned its lesson, was allowed to return to power and a new Anglo-Egyptian treaty was signed. The Second World War necessarily constituted a sort of parenthesis. But a rising tide of struggles resumed on February 21, 1946, with the formation of the worker-student bloc, reinforced in its radicalization by the entry onstage of the Communists and the working-class movement. Once again the Egyptian reactionaries, supported by London, responded with violence and to this end mobilized the Muslim Brotherhood behind a second dictatorship by Sedki Pasha—without, however, being able to silence the protest movement. Elections had to be held in 1950, and the Wafd returned to power. Its repudiation of the 1936 treaty and the inception of guerrilla actions in the Suez Canal Zone were defeated only by setting fire to Cairo (January 1952), an operation in which the Muslim Brotherhood was deeply involved.

A first coup d'état in 1952 by the "Free Officers," and above all a second coup in 1954 by which Nasser took control, was taken by some to "crown" the continual flow of struggles and by others to put it to an end. Rejecting the view of the Egyptian awakening advanced above, Nasserism put forth an ideological discourse that wiped out the whole history of the years 1919 to 1952 in order to push the start of the "Egyptian Revolution" to July 1952. At that time many among the Communists had denounced this discourse and analyzed the coups d'état of 1952 and 1954 as aimed at putting an end to the radicalization of the democratic movement. They were not wrong, since Nasserism took the shape of an anti-imperialist project only after the Bandung Conference of April 1955. Nasserism then contributed all it had to give: a resolutely anti-imperialist international posture (in association with the Pan-Arab and Pan-African movements) and some progressive (but not socialist) social reforms. The whole thing done from above, not only "without democracy," the popular masses being denied any right to organize by and for themselves, but even by "abolishing" any form of political life. This was an invitation to political Islam to fill the vacuum thus created. In only ten short years (1955–65) the Nasserist project used up its progressive potential. Its exhaustion offered imperialism, henceforward led by the United States, the chance to break the movement by mobilizing to that end its regional military instrument: Israel. The 1967 defeat marked the end of the tide that had flowed for a half-century. Its reflux was initiated by Nasser himself, who chose the path of concessions to the Right (the infitah or "opening," an opening to capitalist globalization) rather than the radicalization called for by, among others, the student movement, which held the stage briefly in 1970, shortly before and after the death of Nasser. His successor, Sadat, intensified and extended the rightward turn and integrated the Muslim Brotherhood into his new autocratic system. Mubarak continued along the same path.

Under Nasser, Egypt set up an economic and social system that, though subject to criticism, was at least coherent. Nasser wagered on industrialization as the way out of the colonial international specialization that was confining the country to the role of cotton exporter. His system maintained a division of incomes that favored the expanding middle classes without impoverishing the popular masses. Sadat and Mubarak dismantled the Egyptian productive system, putting in its place a completely incoherent system based exclusively on the profitability of firms, most of which were mere subcontractors for the imperialist monopolies. Supposed high rates of economic growth, much praised for thirty years by the World Bank, were completely meaningless. Egyptian growth was extremely vulnerable. Moreover, such growth was accompanied by an incredible rise in inequality and by unemployment afflicting the majority of the country's youth. This was an explosive situation. It exploded.

During the Bandung and Non-Alignment period (1955–70), the Arab countries were in the forefront of the struggles of the peoples, the nations, and the states of the South for a better future and a less unequal global system. Algeria's FLN and Boumedienne, Nasser's Egypt, the Baas regimes in Iraq and Syria, the South Yemen Republic, shared common characteristics. These were not "democratic" regimes according to Western criteria (they were one-party systems), nor even according to my criteria, which implies positive empowerment of the peoples. But they were nevertheless legitimate in the eyes of their peoples for their actual achievements: mass education, health and other public services, industrialization and guarantees for employment, socially upward mobility, associated with independent initiatives and anti-imperialist postures. Therefore they were continually and fiercely opposed by the Western powers, in particular through repeated Israeli aggressions.

These regimes achieved whatever they could within that framework in a short period, say twenty years, and then ran out of steam, as a result of their internal limits and contradictions. This, coinciding with the breakdown of Soviet power, facilitated the imperialist "neoliberal" offensive. The ruling circles, in order to remain in office, chose to retreat and submit to the demands of neoliberal globalization. The result has been a fast degradation of the social conditions. All that had been achieved in the era of the National Popular State to the benefit of the popular and middle classes was lost in a few years, poverty and mass unemployment the result of the neoliberal policies pursued. Thus the objective conditions for the revolts were created.

The period of retreat lasted, in its turn, almost a half-century. Egypt, submissive to the demands of globalized liberalism and to U.S. strategy, simply ceased to exist as an active factor in regional or global politics. Instead, the major U.S. allies—Saudi Arabia and Israel—occupied the foreground. Israel was then able to pursue its course of expanding colonization of occupied Palestine with the tacit complicity of Egypt and the Gulf countries.

De-politicization of the society due to the modus operandi of the Nasserist regime is behind the rise of political Islam. Note that Nasserism was not the only system that took this approach. Rather, most national-populist regimes of the first wave of awakening in the South had a similar approach in the management of politics. Note also that the existing socialist regimes have also taken this approach, at least after the revolutionary phase, which was democratic in nature, when they solidified their rule. So, the common denominator is the abolition of democratic praxis. And I do not mean to equate democracy with multiparty elections. Rather, I mean the practice of democracy in the proper sense of the word, that is, respect for the plurality of political views and political schemes and for political organizing. Because politicization assumes democracy, democracy does not exist if those who differ in opinion with the authority do not enjoy freedom of expression. The obliteration of the right to organize around different political views and projects eliminated the politicization, which ultimately caused the subsequent disaster.

This disaster has manifested itself in the return to bygone archaic views, religious or otherwise, and is also reflected in the acceptance of the project of the "consumer society" based on solidification of the so-called trend of individualism, which has spread not only within the middle class that benefits from such a pattern of development, but also among the poor masses who call for participating in what appears a minimal welfare—even with its maximum simplicity—in the absence of a credible real alternative. Therefore one must consider this as a legitimate demand from the popular classes. The de-politicization in Islamic societies took a prevailing form manifested in the apparent or superficial "return" to "Islam." Consequently, the discourse of the mosque along with the discourse of the authority became the only ones allowed in Nasser's period, and became even more so during the periods of Sadat and Mubarak. This discourse was used to stop the emergence of an alternative based on the entrenching of a socialist aspiration. Then this "religious" discourse was encouraged by Sadat and Mubarak to accompany and cope with the deteriorating living conditions resulting from the subjugation of Egypt to the requirements of imperialist globalization. This is why I argue that political Islam does not belong to the opposition bloc, as claimed by the Muslim Brotherhood, but is an organic part of the power structure.

The success of political Islam requires further clarification regarding the relationship between the success of imperialist globalization on the one hand, and the rise of the Brotherhood on the other. The deterioration that accompanied this globalization produced proliferation in the activities of the informal sector in economic and social life, which represents the most important sources of income for the majority of people in Egypt (statistics say 60 percent). The Brotherhood's organizations have a real ability to work in these circumstances, so that the success of the Brotherhood in these areas has in turn produced more inflation in these activities and thus ensured its reproduction on a larger scale. The political culture offered by the Brotherhood is known for its great simplicity. As this culture is content with only conferring Islamic "legitimacy" to the principle of private property and the "free market" relations, without considering the nature of the activities concerned, which are rudimentary bazaar activities that are unable to push forward the national economy and lead to its development. Furthermore, the wide provision of funds by the Gulf States has allowed a boom in such activities, pumping in funds in the form of small loans or grants. This is in addition to charity work (clinics, etc.) that has accompanied this inflated sector thanks to the support of the Gulf States. The Gulf States do not intend to contribute to the development of productive capacity in the Egyptian economy (building factories, and so forth), but only to a lumpen-development, since reviving Egypt as a developing state would end the domination of the Gulf States, which are based on the acceptance of the slogan of Islamization of the society; the dominance of the United States, which assumes Egypt is a comprador state infected with worsening poverty; and the domination of Israel, which assumes the impotence of Egypt in the face of Zionist expansion.

The apparent stability of the regime, boasted of by successive U.S. officials like Hillary Clinton, is based on a monstrous police apparatus of 1.2 million men (the army numbering a mere 500,000) free to carry out daily acts of criminal abuse. The imperialist powers claimed that this regime was "protecting" Egypt from the threat of Islamism. This was nothing but a clumsy lie. In reality, the regime had perfectly integrated reactionary political Islam (on the Wahhabite model of the Gulf) into its power structure by giving it control of education, the courts, and the major media, especially television. The sole permitted public speech was that of the Salafist mosques, allowing the Islamists, to boot, to pretend to make up "the opposition." The cynical duplicity of the U.S. establishment's speeches (Obama no less than Bush) was perfectly adapted to its aims. The de facto support for political Islam destroyed the capacity of Egyptian society to confront the challenges of the modern world, bringing about a catastrophic decline in education and research. By occasionally denouncing its "abuses," like assassinations of Copts, Washington could legitimize its military interventions as actions in its self-styled "war against terrorism." The regime could still appear "tolerable" as long as it had the safety valve provided by mass emigration of poor and middle-class workers to the oil-producing countries. The exhaustion of that system (Asian immigrants replacing those from Arabic countries) brought with it the rebirth of opposition movements. The workers' strikes in 2007 (the strongest strikes on the African continent in the past fifty years), the stubborn resistance of small farmers threatened with expropriation by agrarian capital, and the formation of democratic protest groups among the middle classes (like the Kefaya and April 6 movements) foretold the inevitable explosion—expected by Egyptians but startling to "foreign observers." And thus began a new phase in the tide of emancipation struggles, whose directions and opportunities for development we are now called on to analyze.

The history of modern Egypt is that of successive waves of attempts at emergence, designed using essentially the model of a capitalist society. Nonetheless, it is associated with progressive social transformations and advances in democracy, benefiting from a clear vision that the hostility of Western powers must be confronted. The abandonment of these attempts must be largely attributed to this hostility, which has been directed more at Egypt than against the others, particularly modern Turkey.

Egypt entered, in 2011, a new phase in her history. The analysis that I propose consists of a democratic movement, national and popular in its appeal. The strategies of the local reactionary adversary and its outside allies permit one to imagine a multitude of different paths toward emergence. In conclusion to this analysis, one could not say that Egypt is on the path toward emergence. Rather, for the foreseeable future, Egypt will sink into a fatal combination of lumpen-development, powerful political Islam, and submission to the domination of the global imperial system. However, the struggle will continue and will perhaps permit an exit from this impasse and a reinvention of an appropriate road to emergence.

In Turkey and Egypt submission to the comprador economic model, geostrategic alignment with the United States, lumpen-development and pauperization, and the increase in reactionary political Islam trap the societies in a downward spiral. This is because the more a society succumbs to lumpen-development, the more susceptible it is to political Islam. In Iran the duo of lumpen-development and control of society by the Mullahs relegate the country to the downward spiral. Despite the political conflict with Washington, there has not been in Iran a rupture with the pursuit of a political economy analogous to that of a comprador state. It is therefore more necessary than ever to rid oneself of the illusions of transition led by exercising the power of political Islam.

A prevailing media discourse that is extremely naïve contends that the victory of political Islam became inevitable because Islamic self-identity dominates the reality of our societies, and it is a reality that some had rejected, and thus this reality imposed itself on them.

However, this argument completely ignores another reality, namely, that the de-politicization process was deliberate, and without it no political Islam would have been able to impose itself on these societies. Furthermore, this discourse argues that there is no risk from this victory of political Islam, because it is temporary, for the authority emerging from it is doomed to failure and thus public opinion will abandon it. This is as if the Brotherhoods are those who accept the implementation of the principles of democracy even if it works against their interests! However, the regime in Washington apparently adopts this discourse, as does public opinion there, which is manufactured by the media. And there is an ensemble of Egyptian and Arab intellectuals who also became convinced by this discourse, apparently, perhaps opportunistically, or because of lack of clarity in thought.

But this is a mistake. Let it be known that political Islam, in the supposition of taking over the governments, will continue to impose itself if not "forever," at least for a long time (fifty years?). Let us not forget the case of Iran, for example. During this phase of "transition" other nations will continue their march of development, and so we will find ourselves eventually at the bottom of the list. So I don't see the Brotherhood primarily as an "Islamic party"; it is first a reactionary party, and if it managed to take the government, it represents the best security for the imperialist system.

In this chapter I have alluded briefly to China. In the following chapter I give the reasons why its case is unique and why it perhaps represents the only example of emergence in the full sense of the word, unlike the case of other countries (India, Brazil, and others) that have been described as emergent.

REFERENCES

Samir Amin, *Beyond U.S. Hegemony* (London: ZED, 2006), chap. 2.
Wang Hui, *The End of the Revolution* (London: Verso, 2011).
Lin Chun, *The Transformation of Chinese Socialism* (Durham, NC: Duke University Press, 2006).
Lin Chun, *China and Global Capitalism* (Basingstoke, UK: Palgrave Pivot, forthcoming).

3. CHINA: THE EMERGING COUNTRY

THE DEBATES CONCERNING the present and future of China—an "emerging" power—always leave me unconvinced. Some argue that China has chosen, once and for all, the "capitalist road" and intends even to accelerate its integration into contemporary capitalist globalization. They are quite pleased with this and hope only that this "return to normality"— capitalism being the "end of history"—is accompanied by development toward Western-style democracy (multiple parties, elections, human rights). They believe—or need to believe—in the possibility that China shall by this means "catch up" in terms of per capita income to the opulent societies of the West, even if gradually, which I do not believe is possible. The Chinese right shares this point of view. Others deplore this in the name of the values of a "betrayed socialism." Some associate themselves with the dominant expressions of the practice of *China bashing* in the West. Still others—those in power in Beijing—describe the chosen path as "Chinese-style socialism," without being more precise. However, one can discern its characteristics by reading official texts closely, particularly the Five-Year Plans, which are precise and taken quite seriously.

The question of "Is China capitalist or socialist?" is badly posed, too general and abstract for any response to make sense in terms of this absolute alternative. China has actually been following an original path since 1950, and perhaps even since the Taiping Revolution in the nineteenth century. I shall attempt here to clarify the nature of this original path at each of the stages of its development from 1950 till today—2012.

The Agrarian Question

Mao described the nature of the revolution carried out in China by its Communist Party as an anti-imperialist/anti-feudal revolution looking toward socialism. Mao never assumed, after having dealt with imperialism and feudalism, that the Chinese people had "constructed" a socialist society. He always characterized this construction as the first phase of the long path to socialism.

I must emphasize the specific nature of the response given to the agrarian question by the Chinese Revolution. The distributed (agricultural) land was not privatized; it remained the property of the nation represented by village communes, its use given only to rural families. That had not been the case in Russia where Lenin, faced with the fait accompli of the peasant insurrection in 1917, recognized the private property of the beneficiaries of the land distribution.

Why was the implementation of the principle that agricultural land is not a commodity possible in China (and Vietnam)? It is constantly repeated that peasants around the world long for property and that alone. If such had been the case in China, the decision to nationalize the land would have led to an endless peasant war, as was the case when Stalin began forced collectivization in the Soviet Union.

The attitude of the peasants of China and Vietnam (and nowhere else) cannot be explained by a supposed "tradition" in which they are unaware of property. It is the product of an intelligent and exceptional political line implemented by the Communist parties of these two countries.

The Second International took for granted the inevitable aspiration of peasants for property, which were real enough in nineteenth-century Europe. Over the long European transition from feudalism to capitalism (1500–1800), the earlier institutionalized feudal forms of access to the land through rights shared among king, lords, and peasant serfs had gradually been dissolved and replaced by modern bourgeois private property, which treats the land as a commodity—a good that the owner can freely dispose of (buy and sell). The socialists of the Second International accepted this fait accompli of the "bourgeois revolution," even if they deplored it.

They also thought that small peasant property had no future, which belonged to large mechanized agricultural enterprise modeled on industry. They thought that capitalist development by itself would lead to such a concentration of property and to the most effective forms of its exploitation (see Kautsky's writings on this subject). History proved them wrong. Peasant agriculture gave way to capitalist family agriculture in a double sense: one that produces for the market (farm consumption having become insignificant) and one that makes use of modern equipment, industrial inputs, and bank credit. What is more, this capitalist family agriculture has turned out to be quite efficient in comparison with large farms, in terms of volume of production per hectare per worker/year. This observation does not exclude the fact that the modern capitalist farmer is exploited by generalized monopoly capital, which controls the upstream supply of inputs and credit and the downstream marketing of the products. These farmers have been transformed into subcontractors for dominant capital.

Thus (wrongly) persuaded that large enterprise is always more efficient than small in every area—industry, services, and agriculture—the radical socialists of the Second International assumed that the abolition of landed property (nationalization of the land) would allow the creation of large socialist farms (analogous to the future Soviet sovkhozes and kolkhozes). However, they were unable to put such measures to the test since revolution was not on the agenda in their countries, the imperialist centers.

The Bolsheviks accepted these theses until 1917. They contemplated the nationalization of the large estates of the Russian aristocracy, while leaving property in communal lands to the peasants. However, they were subsequently caught unaware by the peasant insurrection, which seized the large estates.

Mao drew lessons from this history and developed a completely different line of political action. Beginning in the 1930s in southern China, during the long civil war of liberation, Mao based the increasing presence of the Communist Party on a solid alliance with the poor and landless peasants (the majority), maintained friendly relations with the middle peasants, and isolated the rich peasants (kulaks) at all stages of the war, without necessarily antagonizing them. The success of this line prepared the large majority of rural inhabitants to accept a solution to their problems that did not require private property in plots of land acquired through distribution. I think that Mao's ideas, and their successful implementation, have their historical roots in the nineteenth-century Taiping Revolution. Mao thus succeeded in realizing what the Bolshevik Party failed to do: establish a solid alliance with the large rural majority. In Russia, the fait accompli of summer 1917 eliminated later opportunities for an alliance with the poor and middle peasants against the rich ones (the kulaks) because the former were anxious to defend their acquired private property and, consequently, preferred to follow the kulaks rather than the Bolsheviks.

This "Chinese specificity"—whose consequences are of major importance—absolutely prevents us from characterizing contemporary China (even today) as "capitalist," because the capitalist road is based on the transformation of land into a commodity.

Present and Future of Petty Production

Once this principle is accepted, the forms of using this common good (the land of the village communities) can be diverse. In order to understand this, we must be able to distinguish petty production from small property. Petty production—peasant and artisanal—dominated production in all past societies. It has retained an important place in modern capitalism, now linked with small property—in agriculture, services, and even certain segments of industry. Certainly in the dominant Triad of the contemporary world (the United States, Europe, and Japan) it is receding. An example of that is the disappearance of small businesses and their replacement by large commercial operations. Yet this is not to say that this change is "progress," even in terms of efficiency, all the more so if the social, cultural, and civilizational dimensions are taken into account. In fact, this is an example of the distortion produced by the domination of rent-seeking generalized monopolies. Hence, perhaps in a future socialism the place of petty production will be called upon to resume its importance. In contemporary China, in any case, petty production—which is not necessarily linked with small property—retains an important place in national production, not only in agriculture, but also in large segments of urban life.

China has experienced quite diverse and even contrasting forms of the use of land as a common good. We need to discuss, on the one hand, efficiency—volume of production from a hectare per worker/year—and, on the other, the dynamics of the transformations set in motion. These forms can strengthen tendencies toward capitalist development, which would end up calling into question the non-commodity status of the land, or can be part of development in a socialist direction. These questions can be answered only through a concrete examination of the forms at issue, as they were implemented in successive moments of Chinese development from 1950 to the present.

At the beginning, in the 1950s, the form adopted was petty family production combined with simpler forms of cooperation for managing irrigation, work requiring coordination, and the use of certain kinds of equipment. And the insertion of such petty family production into a state economy that maintained a monopoly over purchases of produce destined for the market and the supply of credit and inputs, all on the basis of planned prices decided by the central planners.

The experience of the communes that followed the establishment of production cooperatives in the 1970s is full of lessons. It was not necessarily a question of passing from small production to large farms, even if the idea of the superiority of the latter inspired some of its supporters. The essentials of this initiative originated in the aspiration for decentralized socialist construction. The communes not only had responsibility for managing the agricultural production of a large village or a collective of villages and hamlets (this organization itself was a mixture of forms of small family production and more ambitious specialized production), they also provided a framework to attach industrial activities that employed peasants available in certain seasons; articulated productive economic activities with the management of social services (education, health, housing); and began the decentralization of the political administration of the society. Just as the Paris Commune had intended, the socialist state was to become, at least partially, a federation of socialist communes. Undoubtedly, in many respects, the communes were in advance of their time and the dialectic between the decentralization of decision-making powers and the centralization assumed by the omnipresence of the Communist Party did not always operate smoothly. Yet the recorded results are far from disastrous, as the right would have us believe. A commune in the Beijing region, which resisted the order to dissolve the system, continues to record excellent economic results linked with the persistence of high-quality political debates, which disappeared elsewhere. Current (2012) projects of "rural reconstruction," implemented by rural communities in several regions of China, appear to be inspired by the experience of the communes.

The decision to dissolve the communes made by Deng Xiaoping in 1980 strengthened small family production, which remained the dominant form during the three decades following this decision (1980–2012). However, the range of users' rights (for village communes and family units) has expanded considerably. It has become possible for the holders of these land-use rights to "rent" that land out (but never "sell" it), either to other small producers—thus facilitating emigration to the cities, particularly of educated young people who do not want to remain rural residents—or to firms organizing a much larger, modernized farm (never a latifundia, which does not exist in China, but nevertheless considerably larger than family farms). This form is the means for encouraging specialized production (such as good wine, for which China has called on the assistance of experts from Burgundy) or test new scientific methods (GMOs and others).

To "approve" or "reject" the diversity of these systems a priori makes no sense, in my opinion. Once again, the concrete analysis of each of them, both in design and the reality of implementation, is imperative. The fact remains that the inventive diversity of forms of using commonly held land has led to phenomenal results. First of all, in terms of economic efficiency, although urban population has grown from 20 to 50 percent of total population, China has succeeded in increasing agricultural production to keep pace with the gigantic needs of urbanization. This is a remarkable and exceptional result, unparalleled in the countries of the "capitalist" South. It has preserved and strengthened its food sovereignty, even though it suffers from a major handicap: its agriculture feeds 22 percent of the world's population reasonably well while it has only 6 percent of the world's arable land. In addition, in terms of the way (and level) of life of rural populations, Chinese villages no longer have anything in common with what is still dominant elsewhere in the capitalist Third World. Comfortable and well-equipped permanent structures form a striking contrast, not only with the former China of hunger and extreme poverty, but also with the extreme forms of poverty that still dominate the countryside of India or Africa.

The principles and policies implemented (land held in common, support for petty production without small property) are responsible for these unequalled results. They have made possible a relatively controlled rural to urban migration. Compare that with the capitalist road in Brazil, for example. Private property in agricultural land has emptied the countryside of Brazil—today it represents only 11 percent of the country's population. But at least 50 percent of urban residents live in slums (favelas) and survive only thanks to the "informal economy" (including organized crime). There is nothing similar in China, where the urban population is, as a whole, adequately employed and housed, even in comparison with many "developed countries," without even mentioning those where the GDP per capita is at the Chinese level.

The population transfer from the densely populated Chinese countryside (only Vietnam, Bangladesh, and Egypt are similar) was essential. It improved conditions for rural petty production, making more land available. This transfer, although relatively controlled (once again, nothing is perfect in the history of humanity, neither in China nor elsewhere), is perhaps threatening to become too rapid. This is being discussed in China.

Chinese State Capitalism

The first label that comes to mind to describe Chinese reality is "state capitalism." Very well, but this label remains vague and superficial as long as the specific content is not analyzed.

It is indeed capitalism in the sense that the relation to which the workers are subjected by the authorities who organize production is similar to the one that characterizes capitalism: submissive and alienated labor, extraction of surplus labor. Brutal forms of extreme exploitation of workers exist in China, for example, in the coal mines and in the furious pace of the workshops that employ women. This is scandalous for a country that claims to want to move forward on the road to socialism. Nevertheless, the establishment of a state capitalist regime is unavoidable, and will remain so everywhere. The developed capitalist countries will not be able to enter a socialist path (which is not on the visible agenda today) without passing through this first stage. It is the preliminary phase in the potential commitment of any society to liberating itself from historical capitalism on the long route to socialism/communism. Socialization and reorganization of the economic system at all levels, from the firm (the elementary unit) to the nation and the world, require a lengthy struggle during a historical time period that cannot be foreshortened.

Beyond this preliminary reflection, we must concretely describe the state capitalism in question by bringing out the nature and the project of the state concerned, because there is not just one type of state capitalism, but many different types. The state capitalism of France of the Fifth Republic from 1958 to 1975 was designed to serve and strengthen private French monopolies, not to commit the country to a socialist path.

Chinese state capitalism was built to achieve three objectives: (1) construct an integrated and sovereign modern industrial system; (2) manage the relation of this system with rural petty production; and (3) control China's integration into the world system, dominated by the generalized monopolies of the imperialist Triad. The pursuit of these three priority objectives is unavoidable. As a result it permits a possible advance on the long route to socialism, but at the same time it strengthens tendencies to abandon that possibility in favor of pursuing capitalist development pure and simple. It must be accepted that this conflict is both inevitable and always present. The question then is this: Do China's concrete choices favor one of the two paths?

Chinese state capitalism required in its first phase (1954–1980) the nationalization of all companies (combined with the nationalization of agricultural lands), both large and small alike. Then followed an opening to private enterprise, national or foreign, and liberalized rural and urban petty production (small companies, trade, services). However, large basic industries and the credit system established during the Maoist period were not de-nationalized, even if the organizational forms of their integration into a "market economy" were modified. This choice went hand in hand with the establishment of means of control over private initiative and potential partnership with foreign capital. It remains to be seen to what extent these means fulfill their assigned functions or, on the contrary, if they have not become empty shells, collusion with private capital (through "corruption" of management) having gained the upper hand.

Still, what Chinese state capitalism has achieved between 1950 and 2012 is quite simply amazing. It has succeeded in building a sovereign and integrated modern productive system to the scale of this gigantic country, which cannot be compared with that of the United States. It has succeeded in leaving behind the tight technological dependence of its origins (importation of Soviet, then Western models) through the development of its own capacity to produce technological inventions. However, it has not (yet?) begun the reorganization of labor from the perspective of socialization of economic management. The Plan—and not the "opening"—has remained the central means for implementing this systematic construction.

In the Maoist phase of this development planning, the Plan remained imperative in all details: nature and location of new establishments, production objectives, prices. At that stage, no reasonable alternative was possible. I will mention here, without pursuing it further, the interesting debate about the nature of the law of value that underpinned planning in this period. The very success—and not the failure—of this first phase required an alteration of the means for pursuing an accelerated development project. The "opening" to private initiative—beginning in 1980, but above all from 1990—was necessary in order to avoid the stagnation that was fatal to the USSR. Despite the fact that this opening coincided with the globalized triumph of neoliberalism—with all the negative effects of this coincidence, to which I shall return—the choice of a "socialism *of* the market," or better yet, a "socialism *with* the market," as fundamental for this second phase of accelerated development is largely justified, in my opinion.

The results of this choice are, once again, simply amazing. In a few decades, China has built a productive, industrial urbanization that brings together 600 million human beings, two-thirds of whom were urbanized over the last two decades (almost equal to Europe's population!). This is due to the Plan and not to the market. China now has a truly sovereign productive system. No other country in the South (except for Korea and Taiwan) has succeeded in doing this. In India and Brazil there are only a few disparate elements of a sovereign project of the same kind, nothing more.

The methods for designing and implementing the Plan have been transformed in these new conditions. The Plan remains imperative for the huge infrastructure investments required by the project: to house 400 million new urban inhabitants in adequate conditions, and to build an unparalleled network of highways, roads, railways, dams and electric power plants; to open up all or almost all of the Chinese countryside; and to transfer the center of gravity of development from the coastal regions to the continental West. The Plan also remains imperative—at least in part—for the objectives and financial resources of publicly owned enterprises (state, provinces, municipalities). As for the rest, it points to possible and probable objectives for the expansion of small urban commodity production as well as industrial and other private activities. These objectives are taken seriously and the political economic resources required for their realization are specified. On the whole, the results are not too different from the "planned" predictions.

Chinese state capitalism has integrated into its development project visible social (I am not saying "socialist") dimensions. These objectives were already present in the Maoist era: eradication of illiteracy, basic health care for everyone, etc. In the first part of the post-Maoist phase (the 1990s), the tendency was undoubtedly to neglect the pursuit of these efforts. However, it should be noted that the social dimension of the project has since won back its place and, in response to active and powerful social movements, is expected to make more headway. The new urbanization has no parallel in any other country of the South. There are certainly "chic" quarters and others that are not at all opulent, but there are no slums, which have continued to expand everywhere else in the cities of the Third World.

The Integration of China into Capitalist Globalization

We cannot pursue the analysis of Chinese state capitalism—called "market socialism" by the government—without taking into consideration its integration into globalization.

The Soviet world had envisioned a de-linking from the world capitalist system, complementing that de-linking by building an integrated socialist system encompassing the USSR and Eastern Europe. The USSR achieved this de-linking to a great extent, imposed moreover by the West's hostility, even blaming the blockade for its isolation. However, the project of integrating Eastern Europe never advanced very far, despite the initiatives of Comecon. The nations of Eastern Europe remained in uncertain and vulnerable positions, partially de-linked—but on a strictly national basis—and partially open to Western Europe beginning in 1970. There was never a question of a USSR-China integration, not only because Chinese nationalism would not have accepted it, but even more because China's priority tasks did not entail it. Maoist China practiced de-linking in its own way.

Should we say that, by reintegrating itself into globalization beginning in the 1990s, it has fully and permanently renounced de-linking?

China entered globalization in the 1990s by the path of the accelerated development of manufactured exports possible for its productive system, giving first priority to exports whose rates of growth then surpassed those of the growth in GDP. The triumph of neoliberalism favored the success of this choice for fifteen years (from 1990 to 2005). The pursuit of this choice is questionable not only because of its political and social effects, but also because it is threatened by the implosion of neoliberal globalized capitalism, which began in 2007. The Chinese government appears to be aware of this and very early began to attempt a correction by giving greater importance to the internal market and to development of western China.

To say, as one hears ad nauseam, that China's success should be attributed to the abandonment of Maoism (whose "failure" was obvious), the opening to the outside and the entry of foreign capital is quite simply idiotic. The Maoist construction put in place the foundations without which the opening would not have achieved its well-known success. A comparison with India, which has not made a comparable revolution, demonstrates this. To say that China's success is mainly, even "completely," attributable to the initiatives of foreign capital is no less idiotic. It is not multinational capital that built the Chinese industrial system and achieved the objectives of urbanization and the construction of infrastructure. The success is 90 percent attributable to the sovereign Chinese project. Certainly, the opening to foreign capital has fulfilled useful functions: it has increased the import of modern technologies. However, because of its partnership methods, China absorbed these technologies and has now mastered their development. There is nothing similar elsewhere, even in India or Brazil, a fortiori in Thailand, Malaysia, South Africa, and other places.

China's integration into globalization has remained, moreover, partial and controlled (or at least controllable, if one wants to put it that way). China has remained outside of financial globalization. Its banking system is completely national and focused on the country's internal credit market. Management of the yuan is still a matter for China's sovereign decision making. The yuan is not subject to the vagaries of the flexible exchanges that financial globalization imposes. Beijing can say to Washington: "The yuan is our money and your problem," just like Washington said to the Europeans in 1971: "The dollar is our money and your problem."

Moreover, China retains a large reserve for deployment in its public credit system. The public debt is negligible compared with the rates of indebtedness considered intolerable in the United States, Europe, Japan, and many of the countries of the South. China can thus increase the expansion of its public expenditures without serious danger of inflation.

The attraction of foreign capital to China, from which it has benefited, is not behind the success of its project. On the contrary, it is the success of the project that has made investment in China attractive for Western transnationals. The countries of the South that opened their doors much wider than China and unconditionally accepted their submission to financial globalization have not become attractive to the same degree. Transnational capital is not attracted to China to pillage the natural resources of the country nor, without any transfer of technology, to outsource and benefit from low wages for labor; nor to seize the benefits from training and integration of offshore units unrelated to nonexistent national productive systems, as in Morocco and Tunisia; nor even to carry out a financial raid and allow the imperialist banks to dispossess the national savings, as was the case in Mexico, Argentina, and Southeast Asia. In China, by contrast, foreign investments can certainly benefit from low wages and make good profits, on condition that their plans fit into China's and allow technology transfer. In sum, these are "normal" profits, but more can be made if collusion with Chinese authorities permits.

China, Emerging Power

No one doubts that China is an emerging power. One current idea is that China is only attempting to recover the place it had occupied for centuries and lost in the nineteenth century. However, this idea—certainly correct, and flattering, moreover—does not help us much in understanding the nature of this emergence and its real prospects in the contemporary world. Incidentally, those who propagate this general and vague idea have no interest in considering whether China will emerge by rallying to the general principles of capitalism (which they think is probably necessary) or whether it will take seriously its project of "socialism with Chinese characteristics." For my part, I argue that if China is indeed an emerging power, this is precisely because it has not chosen the capitalist path of development pure and simple; and that, as a consequence, if it decided to follow that capitalist path, the project of emergence would be in serious danger of failing.

The thesis that I support implies rejecting the idea that peoples can leap over the necessary sequence of stages; thus China must go through a capitalist development before the question of its possible socialist future is considered. The debate on this question between the different currents of historical Marxism was never concluded. Marx remained hesitant on this question. We know that right after the first European attacks (the Opium Wars), he wrote that the next time you (England) send your armies to China they will be welcomed by a banner saying, "Attention, you are at the frontiers of the bourgeois Republic of China." This is a magnificent intuition and shows confidence in the capacity of the Chinese people to respond to the challenge, but at the same time an error because in fact the banner read: "You are at the frontiers of the People's Republic of China." Yet we know that, concerning Russia, Marx did not reject the idea of skipping the capitalist stage (see his correspondence with Vera Zasulich). Today, one might believe that the first Marx was right and that China is indeed on the route to capitalist development.

But Mao understood—better than Lenin—that the capitalist path would lead to nothing and that the resurrection of China could only be the work of Communists. The Qing emperors at the end of the nineteenth century, followed by Sun Yat Sen and the Kuomintang, had already planned a Chinese resurrection in response to the challenge from the West. However, they imagined no other way than that of capitalism and did not have the intellectual wherewithal to understand what capitalism really is and why this path was closed to China, and to all the peripheries of the world capitalist system for that matter. Mao, independent Marxist spirit, understood this. More than that, Mao understood that this battle was not won in advance—by the 1949 victory—and that the conflict between commitment to the long route to socialism, the condition for China's renaissance, and return to the capitalist fold would occupy the foreseeable future.

Personally, I have always shared Mao's analysis, and I shall return to this subject in some of my thoughts concerning the role of the Taiping Revolution, which I consider to be the distant origin of Maoism, the 1911 revolution in China, and other revolutions in the South at the beginning of the twentieth century, The debates at the beginning of the Bandung period and the analysis of the impasses in which the so-called emergent countries of the South committed to the capitalist path are at an impasse. All these considerations are corollaries of my central thesis concerning the polarization (that is, construction of the center/periphery contrast) immanent to the world development of historical capitalism. This polarization eliminates the possibility for a country from the periphery to "catch up" within the context of capitalism. We must draw the conclusion: if "catching up" with the opulent countries is impossible, something else must be done; it is called "following the socialist path."

China has not followed a particular path since 1980, but since 1950, although this path has passed through phases that are different in many respects. China has developed a coherent, sovereign project that is appropriate for its own needs. This is certainly not capitalism, whose logic requires that agricultural land be treated as a commodity. This project remains sovereign insofar as China remains outside of contemporary financial globalization.

The fact that the Chinese project is not capitalist does not mean that it is socialist, only that it makes it possible to advance on the long road to socialism. Nevertheless, China is also still threatened with a drift that moves it off that road and ends up with a return, pure and simple, to capitalism.

China's successful emergence is completely the result of this sovereign project. In this sense, China is the only authentically emergent country (along with Korea and Taiwan, about which I will say more later). None of the many other countries to which the World Bank has awarded a certificate of emergence is really emergent because none of these countries is persistently pursuing a coherent sovereign project. All subscribe to the fundamental principles of capitalism pure and simple, even in potential sectors of their state capitalism. All have accepted submission to contemporary globalization in all its dimensions, including financial. Russia and India are partial exceptions to this last point, but not Brazil, South Africa and others. Sometimes there are pieces of a "national industry policy," but nothing comparable with the systematic Chinese project of constructing a complete, integrated, and sovereign industrial system (notably in the area of technological expertise).

For these reasons, all these other countries, too quickly characterized as emergent, remain vulnerable, certainly in varying degrees, but always much more than China. For all these reasons, the appearances of emergence—respectable rates of growth, capacities to export manufactured products—are always linked with the processes of pauperization that impact the majority of their populations (particularly the peasantry), which is not the case with China. Certainly the growth of inequality is obvious everywhere, including China, but this observation remains superficial and deceptive. Inequality in the distribution of benefits from a model of growth that nevertheless excludes no one (and is even accompanied with a reduction in pockets of poverty—this is the case in China) is one thing; the inequality connected with a growth that benefits only a minority (from 5 to 30 percent of the population, depending on the case) while the fate of the others remains desperate is another thing. The practitioners of *China bashing* are unaware—or pretend to be unaware—of this decisive difference. The inequality that is apparent from the existence of quarters with luxurious villas, on the one hand, and quarters with comfortable housing for the middle and working classes, on the other, is not the same as the inequality apparent from the juxtaposition of wealthy quarters, middle-class housing, and slums for the majority.

The Gini coefficient is valuable for measuring the changes from one year to another in a system with a fixed structure. However, in international comparisons between systems with different structures, it loses its meaning, like all other measures of macroeconomic magnitudes in national accounts. The emergent countries (other than China) are indeed "emergent markets," open to penetration by the monopolies of the imperialist Triad. These markets allow the latter to extract, to their benefit, a considerable part of the surplus-value produced in the country in question. China is different: it is an emergent nation in which the system makes possible the retention of the majority of the surplus-value produced there.

Korea and Taiwan are the only two examples of an authentic emergence in and through capitalism. These two countries owe this success to geostrategic reasons—the United States allowed them to achieve what it prohibited others from doing. The contrast between the support of the United States to the state capitalism of these two countries and the extremely violent opposition to state capitalism in Nasser's Egypt or Boumedienne's Algeria is, in this account, quite illuminating.

I will not discuss here potential projects of emergence, which appear quite possible in Vietnam and Cuba, or the conditions of a possible resumption of progress in this direction in Russia. Nor will I discuss the strategic objectives of the struggle by progressive forces elsewhere in the capitalist South, in India, Southeast Asia, Latin America, the Arab world, and Africa, which could facilitate moving beyond current impasses and encourage the emergence of sovereign projects that initiate a true rupture with the logic of dominant capitalism.

Great Successes, New Challenges

China has not just arrived at the crossroads; it has been there every day since 1950. Social and political forces from the right and left, active in society and the party, have constantly clashed.

Where does the Chinese right come from? Certainly, the former comprador and bureaucratic bourgeoisies of the Kuomintang were excluded from power. However, over the course of the War of Liberation, entire segments of the middle classes, professionals, functionaries, and industrialists, disappointed by the ineffectiveness of the Kuomintang in the face of Japanese aggression, drew closer to the Communist Party, even joined it. Many of them—but certainly not all—remained nationalists, and nothing more. Subsequently, beginning in 1990 with the opening to private initiative, a new, more powerful right made its appearance. It should not be reduced to "businessmen" who have succeeded and made (sometimes colossal) fortunes, strengthened by their clientele—including state and party officials, who mix control with collusion, even corruption. This success, as always, encourages support for rightist ideas in the expanding educated middle classes. It is in this sense that the growing inequality—even if it has nothing in common with inequality characteristic of other countries in the South—is a major political danger, the vehicle for the spread of rightist ideas, depoliticization, and naïve illusions.

Here I shall make an additional observation that I believe is important: petty production, particularly peasant, is not motivated by rightist ideas, as Lenin thought (although this was accurate in Russian conditions). China's situation contrasts here with that of the ex-USSR. The Chinese peasantry, as a whole, is not reactionary because it is not defending the principle of private property, in contrast with the Soviet peasantry, whom the Communists never succeeded in turning away from supporting the kulaks in defense of private property. On the contrary, the Chinese peasantry of petty producers (without being small property owners) is today a class that does not offer rightist solutions, but is part of the camp of forces agitating for the adoption of the most courageous social and ecological policies. The powerful movement of "renovating rural society" testifies to this. The Chinese peasantry largely stands in the leftist camp, with the working class. The left has its organic intellectuals and it exercises some influence on the state and party apparatuses.

The perpetual conflict between the right and left in China has always been reflected in the successive political lines implemented by the state and party leadership. In the Maoist era, the leftist line did not prevail without a fight. Assessing the progress of rightist ideas within the party and its leadership, a bit like the Soviet model, Mao unleashed the Cultural Revolution to fight it. "Bombard the Headquarters," that is, the party leadership, where the "new bourgeoisie" is forming. However, though the Cultural Revolution met Mao's expectations during the first two years of its existence, it subsequently deviated into anarchy, linked to the loss of control by Mao and the left in the party over the sequence of events. This deviation led to the state and party taking things in hand again, which gave the right its opportunity. Since then, the right remains a strong part of all leadership bodies. Yet the left is present on the ground, restricting the supreme leadership to compromises of the "center"—but is that center right or center left?

To understand the nature of challenges facing China today, it is essential to understand that the conflict between China's sovereign project, such as it is, and North American imperialism and its subaltern European and Japanese allies will increase in intensity to the extent that China continues its success. There are several areas of conflict: China's command of modern technologies, access to the planet's resources, the strengthening of China's military capacities and pursuit of the objective of reconstructing international politics on the basis of the sovereign rights of peoples to choose their own political and economic system. Each of these objectives enters into direct conflict with the objectives pursued by the imperialist Triad.

The objective of U.S. political strategy is military control of the planet, the only way that Washington can retain the advantages that give it hegemony. This objective is being pursued by means of the preventive wars in the Middle East, and in this sense these wars are the preliminary to the preventive (nuclear) war against China, cold-bloodedly envisaged by the North American establishment as possibly necessary "before it is too late." Fomenting hostility to China is inseparable from this global strategy, which is manifest in the support shown for the slaveowners of Tibet and Sinkiang, the reinforcement of the American naval presence in the China Sea, and the unstinting encouragement to Japan to build its military forces. The practitioners of *China bashing* contribute to keeping this hostility alive.

Simultaneously, Washington is devoted to manipulating the situation by appeasing the possible ambitions of China and the other so-called emergent countries through the creation of the G20, which is intended to give these countries the illusion that their adherence to liberal globalization would serve their interests. The G2 (United States/China) is—in this vein—a trap that, in making China the accomplice of the imperialist adventures of the United States, could cause Beijing's peaceful foreign policy to lose all its credibility.

The only possible effective response to this strategy must proceed on two levels: (1) strengthen China's military forces and equip them with the potential for a deterrent response; and (2) tenaciously pursue the objective of reconstructing a polycentric international political system, respectful of all national sovereignties, and, to this effect, act to rehabilitate the UN, now marginalized by NATO. I emphasize the decisive importance of the latter objective, which entails the priority of reconstructing a "front of the South" (Bandung 2?) capable of supporting the independent initiatives of the peoples and states of the South. It implies, in turn, that China becomes aware that it does not have the means for the absurd possibility of aligning with the predatory practices of imperialism (pillaging the natural resources of the planet), since it lacks a military power similar to that of the United States, which in the last resort is the guarantee of success for imperialist projects. China, on the other hand, has much to gain by developing its offer of support for the industrialization of the countries of the South, which the club of imperialist "donors" is trying to make impossible.

The language used by Chinese authorities concerning international questions, restrained in the extreme (which is understandable), makes it difficult to know to what extent the leaders of the country are aware of the challenges analyzed above. More seriously, this choice of words reinforces naïve illusions and depoliticization in public opinion.

The other part of the challenge concerns the question of democratizing the political and social management of the country.

Mao formulated and implemented a general principle for the political management of the new China that he summarized in these terms: rally the left, neutralize (and not eliminate) the right, govern from the center left. In my opinion, this is the best way to conceive of an effective manner for moving through successive advances, understood and supported by the great majority. In this way, Mao gave a positive content to the concept of democratization of society combined with social progress on the long road to socialism. He formulated the method for implementing this: "the mass line"—go down into the masses, learn their struggles, go back to the summits of power. Lin Chun has analyzed with precision the method and the results that the mass line makes possible.

The question of democratization connected with social progress—in contrast with a "democracy" disconnected from social progress, and even frequently connected with social regression—does not concern China alone, but all the world's peoples. The methods that should be implemented for success cannot be summarized in a single formula, valid in all times and places. In any case, the formula offered by Western media propaganda—multiple parties and elections—should quite simply be rejected. Moreover, this sort of "democracy" turns into farce, even in the West, more so elsewhere. The mass line was the means for producing consensus on successive, constantly progressing, strategic objectives. This is in contrast with the "consensus" obtained in Western countries through media manipulation and the electoral farce, which is nothing more than alignment with the requirements of capital.

Yet today, how should China begin to reconstruct the equivalent of a new mass line in new social conditions? It will not be easy because the power of the leadership, which has moved mostly to the right in the Communist Party, bases the stability of its management on depoliticization and the naïve illusions that go along with that. The very success of the development policies strengthens the spontaneous tendency to move in this direction. It is widely believed in China, in the middle classes, that the royal road to catching up with the way of life in the opulent countries is now open, free of obstacles; it is believed that the states of the Triad do not oppose that; American methods are even uncritically admired; etc. This is particularly true for the urban middle classes, which are rapidly expanding and whose conditions of life are incredibly improved. The brainwashing to which Chinese students are subject in the United States, particularly in the social sciences, combined with a rejection of the official unimaginative and tedious teaching of Marxism, have contributed to narrowing the spaces for radical critical debates.

The government in China is not insensitive to the social question, not only because of the tradition of a discourse founded on Marxism, but also because the Chinese people, who learned how to fight and continue to do so, force the government's hand. If, in the 1990s, this social dimension had declined before the immediate priorities of speeding up growth, today the tendency is reversed. At the very moment when the social democratic conquests of social security are being eroded in the opulent West, poor China is implementing the expansion of social security in three dimensions—health, housing, pensions. China's popular housing policy, vilified by the *China bashing* of the European right and left, would be envied, not only in India or Brazil, but equally in the distressed areas of Paris, London or Chicago!

Social security and the pension system already cover 50 percent of the urban population (which has increased, recall, from 200 to 600 million inhabitants) and the Plan (still carried out in China) anticipates increasing the covered population to 85 percent in the coming years. Let the journalists of *China bashing* give us comparable examples in the "countries embarked on the democratic path," which they continually praise. Nevertheless, the debate remains open on the methods for implementing the system. The left advocates the French system of distribution based on the principle of solidarity between these workers and different generations—which prepares for the socialism to come—while the right, obviously, prefers the odious American system of pension funds, which divides workers and transfers the risk from capital to labor.

However, the acquisition of social benefits is insufficient if it is not combined with democratization of the political management of society, with its re-politicization by methods that strengthen the creative invention of forms for the socialist/communist future.

Following the principles of a multiparty electoral system as advocated ad nauseam by Western media and the practitioners of *China bashing*, and defended by "dissidents" presented as authentic "democrats," does not meet the challenge. On the contrary, the implementation of these principles could only produce in China, as all the experiences of the contemporary world demonstrate (in Russia, Eastern Europe, the Arab world), the self-destruction of the project of emergence and social renaissance, which is the actual objective of advocating these principles, masked by an empty rhetoric: "There is no other solution than multiparty elections." Yet it is not sufficient to counter this bad solution with a fallback to the rigid position of defending the privilege of the party, itself sclerotic and transformed into an institution devoted to recruitment of officials for state administration. Something new must be invented.

The objectives of re-politicization and creation of conditions favorable to the invention of new responses cannot be obtained through propaganda campaigns. They can only be promoted through social, political, and ideological struggles. This implies the preliminary recognition of the legitimacy of these struggles and legislation based on the collective rights of organization, expression, and proposing legislative initiatives. That implies, in turn, that the party itself is involved in these struggles; in other words, reinvents the Maoist formula of the mass line. Re-politicization makes no sense if it is not combined with procedures that encourage the gradual conquest of responsibility by workers in the management of their society at all levels—company, local, national. A program of this sort does not exclude recognition of the rights of the individual person. On the contrary, it supposes their institutionalization. Its implementation would make it possible to reinvent new ways of using elections to choose leaders.

SOME NOTES ON THIS CHAPTER

This chapter owes much to the debates organized in China (November–December 2012) by Lau Kin Chi (Linjang University, Hong Kong), in association with the South West University of Chongqing (Wen Tiejun), Renmin and Xinhua Universities of Beijing (Dai Jinhua, Wang Hui), the CASS (Huang Ping), and to meetings with groups of activists from the rural movement in the provinces of Shanxi, Shaanxi, Hubei, Hunan, and Chongqing. I extend to all of them my thanks and hope that this paper will be useful for their ongoing discussions. It also owes much to my reading of the writings of Wen Tiejun and Wang Hui.

China bashing. This phrase refers to the favored sport of Western media of all tendencies—including the left, unfortunately—that consists of systematically denigrating, even criminalizing, everything done in China. China exports cheap junk to the poor markets of the Third World (this is true), a horrible crime. However, it also produces high-speed trains, airplanes, satellites, whose marvelous technological quality is praised in the West. China bashers seem to think that the mass construction of housing for the working class is nothing but the abandonment of workers to slums and liken "inequality" in China (working-class houses are not opulent villas) to that in India (opulent villas side-by-side with slums), etc. *China bashing* panders to the infantile opinion found in some currents of the powerless Western "left": if it is not the communism of the twenty-first century, it is a betrayal! *China bashing* participates in the systematic campaign of maintaining hostility toward China, in view of a possible military attack. This is nothing less than a question of destroying the opportunities for an authentic emergence of a great people of the South.

REFERENCES

The Chinese Path and the Agrarian Question

Karl Kautsky, *On the Agrarian Question*, 2 vols. (1899; repr., Winchester, MA: Zwan Publications, 1988).

Samir Amin, "Forerunners of the Contemporary World: The Paris Commune (1871) and the Taiping Revolution (1851–1864)," *International Critical Thought*, CASS, Beijing, vol. 3, no. 2, 2013.

Samir Amin, "The 1911 Revolution in a World Historical Perspective: A Comparison with the Meiji Restoration and the Revolutions in Mexico, Turkey and Egypt" (published in Chinese in 1990).

Samir Amin, *Ending the Crisis of Capitalism or Ending Capitalism?* (Oxford: Pambazuka Press, 2011), chap. 5, "The Agrarian Question."

Contemporary Globalization, the Imperialist Challenge

Samir Amin, *A Life Looking Forward: Memoirs of an Independent Marxist* (London and New York: Zed Books, 2006), chap. 7, "Deployment and Erosion of the Bandung Project."

Samir Amin, *The Law of Worldwide Value* (New York: Monthly Review Press, 2010), "Initiatives from the South," section 4, 121ff.

Samir Amin, *Beyond U.S. Hegemony* (London and New York: Zed Books, 2006), esp. "The Project of the American Ruling Class"; "China, Market Socialism?"; "Russia, Out of the Tunnel?"; "India, A Great Power?"; "Multipolarity in the 20th Century."

Samir Amin, *Obsolescent Capitalism* (London and New York: Zed Books, 2003), chap. 5, "The Militarization of the New Collective Imperialism."

André Gunder Frank, *ReOrient: Global Economy in the Asian Age* (Berkeley: University of California Press, 1998).

Yash Tandon, *Ending Aid Dependence* (Oxford: Fahamu, 2008).

The Democratic Challenge

Samir Amin, "The Democratic Fraud and the Universalist Alternative," *Monthly Review* 62/5 (October 2011): 29–45.

Lin Chun, *The Transformation of Chinese Socialism* (Durham, NC: Duke University Press, 1996).

4. IMPLOSION OF THE EUROPEAN SYSTEM

MAJORITY OPINION IN EUROPE holds that Europe has all it takes to become an economic and political power comparable to, and consequently independent of, the United States. Simple addition of its component populations and GDPs makes that seem obvious. As for me, I believe that Europe suffers from three major handicaps that rule out such a comparison.

First, the northern part of the American continent—the United States and what I call its external province, Canada—is endowed with natural resources incomparably greater than the part of Europe to the west of Russia, as is shown by Europe's dependence on imported energy.

Second, Europe is made up of a good number of historically distinct nations whose diversity of political cultures, even though this diversity is not necessarily marked by national chauvinism, has sufficient weight to exclude recognition of a "European people" on the model of the United States' "American people." We will return to this important matter.

In the third place (and this is the main ground excluding such a comparison) capitalist development in Europe was and remains uneven, whereas American capitalism has developed in a fairly uniform way throughout the Northern American area, at least since the Civil War. Europe, to the west of historic Russia (which includes Ukraine and Belarus), is itself composed of three unequally developed sets of capitalist societies.

Historic capitalism—that is to say, the form of the capitalist mode of production that has become established on a world scale—took shape beginning in the sixteenth century in the London-Amsterdam-Paris triangle and attained its completed form with the political French Revolution and the English Industrial Revolution. This model, which was to become prevalent in the dominant capitalist centers up until the contemporary epoch (liberal capitalism, as Wallerstein called it) expanded in the United States vigorously and rapidly after the Civil War, which put an end to the dominant position of slave power, and also expanded rapidly, later, in Japan. In Europe, after 1870, the model expanded just as rapidly in Germany and Scandinavia. The European core (Great Britain, France, Germany, the Netherlands, Belgium, Switzerland, Austria, and Scandinavia) has now come under the economic, political, and social sway of its own generalized (as I call them) monopolies, which, starting from earlier forms of monopoly capitalism, attained that status in the 1975–90 period.

Still, the generalized monopolies proper to this European region are not "European"; they are still strictly "national," that is to say, German, British, Swedish, etc., even though their businesses are trans-European and even transnational (carried out on a worldwide scale). The same is the case with the contemporary generalized monopolies of the United States and Japan, which along with those of the major European economies, constitute the first level of generalized monopolies. In my commentary on the impressive research work that has been done on this subject, I have emphasized the decisive importance of this conclusion.

The second level involves Italy, Spain, and Portugal in which that same dominant model—currently, that of generalized-monopoly capitalism— only took shape much more recently, after the Second World War. Because of this, these societies retain peculiarities in their forms of economic and political governance that obstruct their rise to equality with the others.

But the third level, comprising the countries of the former "socialist (Soviet-style) world" and Greece, is not the base for any generalized monopolies proper to their own national societies (Greek shipowners being a possible exception, though their status as "Greeks" is highly questionable). Until the Second World War, all these societies were far from constituting developed capitalist societies like those of the European core. Afterward, Soviet-style socialism suppressed still further their embryonic national capitalist bourgeoisies, replacing their rule with a state capitalism having social, if not socialist, features. Having become reintegrated into the capitalist world through membership in the European Union and NATO, these countries thenceforward shared the situation of others in peripheral capitalism, not ruled by their own national generalized monopolies but subject to those of the European core.

This heterogeneity of Europe strictly excludes comparison with the United States/Canada ensemble. But, you might ask, can't this heterogeneity be made to disappear gradually—precisely through the construction of Europe? That is the prevailing opinion in Europe; I disagree, however, and will return to this matter.

Is Europe to Be Compared to the American Dual Continent?

My belief is that it is more realistic to compare Europe to the American dual continent (United States/Canada on one side, Latin America and the Caribbean on the other) than to Northern America alone. The American dual continent constitutes an ensemble within world capitalism characterized by the contrast between its central and dominant north and its peripheral and subordinate South. This domination, which the rising American power of the nineteenth century (having in 1823 proclaimed its ambitions in the Monroe Doctrine) shared with its British competitor (then hegemonic on a world scale), is now mainly exercised by Washington, whose generalized monopolies have broad control over economic and political life south of its border despite recent combative advances that might call its domination into question. The analogy with Europe is evident. The European East is in a peripheral situation of subordination to the European West analogous to the characteristic status of Latin America in relation to the United States.

But this, like all analogies, has its limits, and to ignore them would lead to wrong conclusions about what futures are possible and what the effective strategies are for opening the road to the best of those futures. On two levels difference, rather than analogy, prevails. Latin America is an immense continent endowed with fabulous natural resources—water, land, minerals, petroleum, and natural gas. In no way is Eastern Europe comparable on that level. Moreover, Latin America is likewise much less heterogeneous relative to Eastern Europe: two related languages (though there are many surviving Indian tongues), little national chauvinistic hostility among neighbors. But these differences, however important they might be, are scarcely our major motive for not going on with a simplified analogical reasoning.

U.S. domination over its American South is mainly exerted through economic means, as shown by the model of a Pan-American common market promoted by Washington (though U.S. efforts to impose it are currently at a standstill). Even the part of this model, NAFTA, which is already in effect and annexes a subordinated Mexico to the big North American market, does not institutionally challenge Mexico's political sovereignty. There is nothing naïve about this observation. I am well aware that there are no sealed barriers separating economic methods from those operating on the political level. The Organization of American States has rightly been considered by Latin American opposition forces to be "the United States' Colonial Office," and the list of U.S. interventions, whether military (as in the Caribbean) or in the form of support to a coup d'état, is long enough to prove that.

The institutional form of the relationship among states of the European Union stems from a broader and more complex logic. There is indeed a sort of West European Monroe Doctrine—"Eastern Europe is part of Western Europe." But that is not all there is to it. The European Union is no longer merely a "common market" as it was at its start, originally limited to six countries and then successively extended to others in Western Europe. Since the Maastricht Treaty it has become a political project. Certainly this political project was conceived to further the larger project of having the generalized monopolies manage the societies involved. But it is capable of becoming an arena for conflicts and for challenging those projects and their established methods of implementation. The European institutions are supposed to link the peoples of the Union and set forth several means toward that end, like weighting the representation of states in the European Parliament according to their populations rather than their GDPs. Because of this the prevailing opinion in Europe, including that of most leftists critical of its institutions as presently structured, clings to the hope that "another Europe" is possible.

Before discussing theses and hypotheses about possible alternative futures for the construction of Europe, it seems necessary to go into some discussion of Atlanticism and imperialism, and of European identity.

Europe, or Atlanticist and Imperialist Europe?

Great Britain is more Atlanticist than it is European, deriving this posture from its former position as imperialist hegemon—even though that heritage has now dwindled to the privileged position held by the City of London in the globalized financial system. Therefore, Great Britain subordinates its very special sort of membership in the European Union to the priority it maintains for the institutionalization of an economic and financial Euro-Atlantic market, which prevails over any wish to participate actively in the political construction of Europe.

But it is not only Great Britain that is Atlanticist. The continental European states are no less so, despite their seeming intention to construct a political Europe. Proof of that is given by the central position of NATO in this political construction. That a military alliance with a country outside the Union has been integrated de facto into the "European constitution" constitutes an unparalleled anomaly. For some European countries (Poland, Hungary, the Baltic states) NATO's protection—that is, that of the United States—against their "Russian enemy" (!) is more important than their adhesion to the European Union.

The persistence of Atlanticism and the worldwide expansion of NATO's field of operation after the disappearance of the supposed "Soviet menace" result from what I have analyzed as the emergence of the collective imperialism of the Triad (United States, Europe, Japan), that is, of the dominant centers of generalized-monopoly capitalism who intend to remain dominant despite the rise of emergent states. It is a matter of a relatively recent transformation of the imperialist system, which had previously, and traditionally, been based on conflict among the imperialist powers. The cause for the emergence of this collective imperialism is the need for united confrontation of the challenge by the peripheral peoples and states of Asia, Africa, and Latin America eager to escape from their subordination.

The European imperialist segment at issue involves only Western Europe, all of whose states have always in the modern period been imperialist whether or not they held colonies, since they have and always have had a share in the imperialist rent. Contrariwise, the Eastern European states have no access to it since they have no national generalized monopolies of their own. They have swallowed the illusion, however, that they have a right to it just because of their "Europeanness." Who knows if they will ever be able to get rid of that illusion?

Imperialism having become collective, and remaining so hencefor-ward, shares in regard to the South but a single common policy—that of the Triad—which is a policy of permanent aggression against those peoples and states that dare to call into question its special system of globalization. And collective imperialism has a military leader, if not a hegemon: the United States. It is understood, then, that neither the European Union nor any of its component states any longer has a "foreign policy." The facts show that there is but a single reality: alignment behind whatever Washington (perhaps in agreement with London) decides on its own. Viewed from the South, Europe is nothing else but the uncondi-tional ally of the United States. And though there may be some illusions about this in Latin America—no doubt because hegemony there is exer-cised brutally by the United States alone and not by its subaltern European allies—that is not the case in Asia and Africa. The power holders in the emerging countries know it: those in charge of the other countries in the two continents accept their status as submissive compradors. For all, only Washington counts, not a Europe that might as well not exist at all.

Is There a European Identity?

This time the viewpoint from which this question is to be considered is internal to Europe. For from an external viewpoint—that of the broad South—yes, indeed, "Europe" seems to be a reality. For the peoples of Asia and Africa, whose languages and religions are "non-European" even when that reality has been attenuated by missionary conversions to Christianity or by adopting the official language of the former coloniz-ers, the Europeans are the "Other." Matters are different in Latin America, which, like Northern America, results from the construction of the "other Europe," the New World, linked as a necessity to the formation of historic capitalism.

The question of European identity can only be discussed by looking at Europe as seen from inside. But the theses affirming and denying the real-ity of this identity clash, in polemics that lead each side to bend the stick too far in its own favor. So some evoke Christianity, although one should talk about Catholic, Protestant, and Orthodox Christianities and not pass by the far from negligible numbers of those with no religious practice and even no religious belief at all. Others will point out that a Spaniard is more at ease with an Argentine than with a Lithuanian, that a Frenchman will understand an Algerian better than she will a Bulgarian, that the English move more freely in the parts of the world where people share their language than in Europe. The ancestral Greco-Roman civilization, whether as it was or as it was reconstructed, ought to make Latin and Greek, rather than English, the official languages of Europe (as they were in the Middle Ages). The eighteenth-century Enlightenment scarcely involved more than the London-Amsterdam-Paris triangle even though it was exported as far as Prussia and Russia. Representative electoral democracy is still very insecure and too recent to see its origins as going back to the formation of Europe's visibly diverse political cultures.

There is no difficulty in showing that the still-present power of national identities in Europe. France, Germany, Spain, and Great Britain were all formed through centuries of bitter warfare. Though the insignificant prime minister of Luxembourg can say that his fatherland (or that of his bank?) is Europe, no French president, German chancellor, or British prime minister would dare to say anything so stupid. But does there really have to be a common identity for there to be a legitimate project of regional political integration? I hold that to be in no way the case. Provided that the diversity of identities (call them national) be recognized and that the serious reasons underlying the common will for a political construction be set forth precisely. This principle is not valid merely for Europeans: it is equally so for the peoples of the Caribbean, of Iberian America, of the Arab world, of Africa. One need not believe in Arabism or Negritude to accept an Arab or African project as fully legitimate. Unfortunately, the "Europeanists" do not behave with such intelligence. The great majority of them think it enough to call themselves "supranational" or "antisovereigntist," which is at best meaningless and may even clash with reality. Therefore, my discussion of the viability of a European political project will not be based on the shifting sands of "identity" but on the firm ground of the stakes at issue and the institutional forms for their management.

Is the European Union Viable?

The question is not whether "a" European project (which project? to do what?) would be possible (the answer, obviously, is yes) but whether the currently established project is viable or could be transformed to make it viable. I give no heed to the right-wing "Europeanists," those who in submission to the demands of generalized-monopoly capitalism accept the European Union essentially as is and care only to provide a solution to its present "conjunctural" difficulties, which I maintain are not conjunctural at all. I care only about the arguments of those who claim that "another Europe is possible," including the advocates of a reformed human-faced capitalism, as well as those who share a perspective of socialist transformation for Europe and the world.

Central to the debate is the nature of the crisis pervading Europe and the world. And, as far as Europe is concerned, the upstage crisis of the Eurozone and the backstage crisis of the European Union are inseparable.

At least since the Maastricht Treaty and, in my opinion, since much earlier, the construction of the European Union and of the Eurozone have been conceived and designed as components for the construction of so-called liberal globalization, construction of a system to assure the exclusive domination of generalized-monopoly capitalism. In this context the necessary starting point is analysis of the contradictions that make this project (and therefore the European project included in it) unviable.

But it will be said, in unconditional defense of "a" European project, the project that has the advantage of existing, of already being in place: it can be transformed. To be sure it can—in abstract theory. But what conditions might allow that? I think it would take a double miracle: (1) that the transnational European construction recognize the reality of national sovereignties, the diversity of interests at stake, and organize its institutional functioning on that basis; and (2) that capitalism—insofar as it maintains the general framework of its way of governing its economy and society—be constrained to work in a way different from that dictated by its own logic, which is now that of domination by the generalized monopolies. I see no indication that the majority of Europeanists are able to take account of these requirements. Nor do I see the left minority, who do take account of them, as able to mobilize political and social forces capable of inverting the conservatism of the established Europeanism. Which is why

I conclude that the European Union can be nothing else than what it is, and as such is unviable. The Eurozone crisis shows how impossible it is for this project to be viable.

The "European" project as defined by the Maastricht Treaty and the Eurozone project were sold to public opinion by a propaganda campaign that can only be described as imbecilic and disingenuous. Some—the (relatively) privileged peoples of opulent Western Europe—were told that by erasing national sovereignties an end would be put to the hate-filled wars that had bloodied the continent (and the success of that claptrap is easily understood). It was served up with a sauce: the friendship of the great American democracy, the common struggle for democracy in that big backward South—a new form of acceptance for the old imperialist postures—etc. The others—the poor devils of the East—were promised opulence through "catching up" with Western standards of living.

Both—in their majorities—swallowed this claptrap. In the East they believed, it seems, that adhesion to the European Union would enable that notorious "catch-up," a good bargain indeed. But the price they paid—perhaps as punishment for having accepted regimes practicing the Soviet-style socialism called communism—was a painful structural adjustment lasting several years. Adjustment—that is, "austerity" (for workers, not for billionaires)—was imposed. But its payoff was a social disaster. And so Eastern Europe became the periphery of Western Europe. A recent serious study told us that 80 percent of Romanians reckon that "in the Ceausescu era things were better" (!) Could anyone look for a better sign of de-legitimization for the supposed democracy character-izing the European Union? Will the peoples involved learn their lesson? Will they understand that the logic of capitalism is not that of "catching up" but the contrary, that of deepening inequalities? Who knows!

That Greece is today at the heart of the conflict is both because Greece is part of the Eurozone and because its people hoped to escape the fate of the other ex-"socialist" peripheral Balkan countries. The Greeks (I know not precisely what that name means) thought (or hoped?) that having avoided the misfortune of being governed by "communists" (powerful in the heroic times of the Second World War) and that by grace of the colo-nels (!), they would not have to pay the price imposed on the rest of the Balkans. Europe and the euro would work differently for them. European solidarity, and especially that of the Eurozone partners, however feebly it showed elsewhere (where the crime of communism was to be punished), would act in their favor.

The Greeks are stuck with the outcome of their naïve illusions. They should know now that the system will reduce their status to that of their Balkan neighbors, Bulgaria and Albania. For the logic of the Eurozone is no different from that of the European Union; on the contrary, it reinforces its violence. In a general fashion the logic of capitalist accumulation produces an accentuation of the inequality among nations (it is at the source of the construction of the core/periphery contrast), and accumulation dominated by the generalized monopolies reinforces still more this immanent tendency of the system. Against this, it will be claimed that the European Union's institutions provide the means to correct intra-European inequalities through appropriate financial support directed to the laggard countries within the Union. And this is believed by public opinion in general. In reality, this support (that except for agriculture, which will not be discussed here, is especially devoted to the construction of modern infrastructure) is too insufficient to permit any catching-up. But, even graver, it facilitates penetration by the generalized monopolies and so strengthens the tendency to unequal development through a greater opening of the economies involved. Further, this assistance aims to reinforce certain sub-national regions (Bavaria, Lombardy, and Catalonia, for example) and thereby to weaken the capability of national states to resist the monopolies' diktats.

The Eurozone was designed to aggravate still further that movement. Its fundamental nature is defined by the statute of the European Central Bank, which is forbidden to lend to national governments (and even to a supranational European state were one to exist, which is not the case), but lends exclusively to banks—at a ridiculously low rate—which, in turn, draw from their investments in national bonds a rental income that has reinforced the domination of the generalized monopolies. What is called the financialization of the system is inherent in the strategy of those monopolies. From its inception I had analyzed this system as non-viable, destined to collapse as soon as capitalism would be stricken by a serious crisis. Which is happening before our eyes. I had maintained that the only alternative that might support a gradual and solid European construction required maintenance of national currencies linked in a system of defined exchange rates conceived as a seriously negotiated structure of exchange rates and industrial policies. A system designed to last until, eventually and much later, maturation of its political cultures would allow the establishment of a confederal European state above, but not annihilating, the various national states.

And so the Eurozone has gone into a foreseeable crisis that really threatens its existence, as has finally been admitted even in Brussels. For there is no sign that the European Union has become able to carry out any radical self-criticism that would imply adoption of a different system of currency regulation and abandonment of the liberalism inherent to the treaties still in force.

Those responsible for the bankruptcy of the European project are not its victims—the fragile countries of the European periphery—but, to the contrary, the countries (which is to say, the ruling classes of those countries), foremost among them Germany, that have been the beneficiaries of the system. This makes the insults against the Greek people even more odious. A lazy people? Tax cheats? Mme Lagarde forgets that the cheaters in question are the shipowners protected by (IMF-supported) globalization's freedoms.

My argument is not based on recognizing conflicts among nations, even though things seem to be happening that way. It is based on recognition of the conflict between the generalized monopolies (themselves based only in the countries of the European center) and the workers of the European centers and peripheries alike, even though the costs of the austerity imposed on both have more markedly devastating effects in the peripheral rather than the central countries. The "German model," praised by all Europe's rightist political forces, as well as by a good part of the left, has worked successfully in Germany thanks to the relative docility of its workers who agree to salary levels 30 percent lower than those of the French. This docility is largely behind the success of German exports and the powerful growth of the rents that the German generalized monopolies profit from. Everyone should understand how this model enchants the unconditional defenders of capital.

Thus the worst is still to come: in one way or another, abruptly or gradually, the European project is to be split apart, starting with the Eurozone. Then it's back to the starting line: the 1930s. We would have a mark zone limited to Germany and the countries it dominates on its eastern and southern borders, the Dutch and Scandinavians autonomous but willing to conform, a Great Britain distanced even more from the vicissitudes of continental politics by its Atlanticism, an isolated France (as with de Gaulle? or Vichy?), and a Spain and an Italy unsure and volatile. We would have the worst of both worlds: national European societies submissive to the dictates of the generalized monopolies and the accompanying globalized "liberalism" on the one hand, and on the other, their ruling political forces even more reliant, to the measure of their powerlessness, on "nationalist" demagogy. That sort of political rule would multiply the opportunities of the extreme right. We would have (do we already have?) Pilsudskis, Horthys, Baltic barons, Mussolini and Franco revivalists, Maurassians. The apparently "nationalist" speeches of the extreme rightists are lies, because these political forces (or, at least, their leaders) not only accept capitalism in general but also the only form it can take, that of generalized-monopoly capitalism. An authentic "nationalism" today can only be populist in the true sense of that term: serving, not deceiving, the people. At this time, the word *nationalism* must itself be used cautiously, and perhaps it would be better to replace it with "internationalism of peoples and workers." Contrariwise, the rhetoric of those rightists reduces their nationalist theme to violent chauvinist excesses to be used against immigrants and Gypsies, blamed as the source of the disasters. Nor does this right fail to include in its hatred the "poor," held responsible for their poverty and accused of abusing the benefits of "welfarism."

That is what stubborn insistence on defending the European project even in the face of the gale leads to: its destruction.

Is There a Less Distressing Alternative? Are We Headed Toward a New Wave of Progressive Social Transformations?

Yes, indeed, because in principle more than one alternative still exists. But the conditions for one or another of the possible alternatives to become a reality need to be spelled out. It is impossible to return to a previous stage of capitalist development, to a period before the centralization of capitalist control. We can only go forward, that is to say, in starting from the actual stage of centralization of capitalist control, understanding that the time has come for "expropriation of the expropriators." No other viable perspective is possible. That being said, this proposition does not exclude undertaking struggles which, from stage to stage, go in that direction. On the contrary, it requires the identification of a strategic aim for each stage and the implementation of effective tactics. To do without this preoccupation with stage-adapted strategies and tactics of action is to condemn oneself merely to repeating facile and impotent slogans like "Down with Capitalism!"

In this spirit and in regard to Europe an initial effective move, which is perhaps already taking shape, starts from a challenge to the so-called austerity policies that, moreover, are linked to the rise of the authoritarian, anti-democratic policies required by them. The aim of restarting economic growth, despite the ambiguity of that term (restarting with which activities? and by what means?), is quite naturally linked to it.

But it must be recognized that this first move will clash with the euro's established system of currency management by the ECB (European Central Bank). For that reason I see no possibility to avoid "leaving the euro" through restoration of monetary sovereignty to the European states. Then and only then can a space for maneuver be opened, requiring negotiation among European partners and, by that very fact, revision of the legal texts structuring the European institutions. Then and only then could measures be taken adumbrating a socialization of the monopolies. I envisage, for example, a separation of banking functions and even definitive nationalization of the troubled banks, a lightening of the grip of the monopolies over small and medium businesses and farmers, the adoption of strongly progressive tax codes, of expropriating the facilities of runaway companies in favor of their workers and local governments, of diversifying the number of commercial, industrial, and financial trade partners through opening negotiations, notably with the emerging countries of the South, etc. All these measures require assertion of national economic sovereignty and therefore require disobedience to the European rules forbidding them. For it is obvious to me that political conditions allowing such moves will never simultaneously exist throughout the European Union. There will be no such miracle. So we must accept starting wherever we can, in one or several countries. I remain convinced that once the process has gotten under way it will quickly snowball.

To these propositions (whose formulation, in part at least, has been initiated by President François Hollande) the political forces in service to the generalized monopolies are already counterposing propositions that would deprive them of any significance: "restart growth by making all and sundry more competitive while respecting the openness and transparency of the markets." This discourse is not only that of Merkel; it is likewise that of her social-democratic opponents and of ECB president Draghi. But it must be known—and said—that "open and transparent markets" do not exist. The markets, opaque by nature, are the domain of commercially conflicting monopolies. We are dealing with a disingenuous rhetoric that must be denounced as such. Trying to improve governance of the markets after having accepted them in principle—by proposing rules for their "regulation"—leads to nothing effective. It is to ask of the generalized monopolies—beneficiaries of the system they themselves dominate—that they act against their own interests. They know how to nullify the regulatory rules that supposedly would be imposed on them.

The September 2012 decisions were aimed at escape from the Euro crisis (by setting up a European Solidarity Fund with already allocated monies, by considering the eventual issue of Eurobonds, and by having the ECB promise to make, if necessary, massive open-market purchases to support the prices of Eurozone-government bonds) but they not only came too late—and too little in volume to measure up to the demands of the situation—they were designed as components of an austerity strategy that is sure to preclude any beneficial results from them. Austerity leads to the increase, not the reduction, of national debt—it is pure stupidity to think otherwise. This principled policy, conceptually bounded by the existing financial system—that is to say, conceived in submission to the "expectations" of the generalized and financialized monopolies—is fated to leave open the way to implosion's descending spiral.

Moreover, this principled policy is based on the negation of national sovereignties—those of the European states—even though the conditions for their replacement by a sovereign European state do not exist and will not exist for the foreseeable future. But refusing sovereignty to the states means nothing less than replacing their sovereignty with that of the monopolies. Without national sovereignty no democracy is possible. This is amply shown by the repeated refusal of the European Union to recognize majority opinions expressed in elections and referendums whenever that would be displeasing to monopoly capital!

For this reason, every people in every region of the world demands that respect for national sovereignty be restored. Without such respect, international law is flouted and its place taken by the "right" of imperialist powers to intervene in the affairs of nations that refuse to yield to the dictates of globalized monopoly-capital. Without respect for national sovereignty no democratic and progressive alternative is possible, neither in Europe nor elsewhere.

The twentieth century was not only marked by wars of a violence never before known, resulting in large part from the conflict among imperialisms (of which there were then several). It was also marked by immense revolutionary movements among the nations and peoples then peripheral to the capitalism of that time. These revolutions transformed Russia, Asia, Africa, and Latin America at an accelerated pace and thus provided the major dynamic factor in the transformation of the world. But at the core of the imperialist system, they found only a feeble echo at best. The pro-imperialist reactionary forces kept their grip on political control over the societies in what has become the Triad of contemporary collective imperialism, allowing them to pursue their policies of "containment" and then of "rolling back" that first wave of victorious struggles for the emancipation of the majority of human beings. It was that deficiency of internationalism among workers and peoples that is at the source of the twentieth century's double drama: the exhaustion of the forward movement begun in the peripheries (the first experiments with a socialist perspective, the passage from anti-imperialist liberation to social liberation) and the European socialist movements going over to the camp of capitalism/imperialism with the drift of social-democracy into social liberalism.

But the triumph of capitalism—that of the generalized monopolies—will only prove to have lasted for a short time (1980–2010?). Democratic and social struggles taking place throughout the world, like certain policies among emerging states, call into question the system of domination by the generalized monopolies and adumbrate a second wave of global transformation. These struggles and conflicts involve every society on the planet, in the North as in the South.

For to maintain its power, contemporary capitalism is compelled to attack simultaneously the states, nations, and workers of the South (to super-exploit their labor power and to pillage their natural resources) and the workers of the North, who are forced to compete with those of the South. So the objective conditions for an international convergence of struggles do exist. But from the existence of objective conditions to their activation by subjective social agents of transformation there remains a distance still to be crossed. We have no intention to settle this question with a few big, facile, and empty phrases. Deep study of the conflicts between emerging states and the imperialism of the Triad and of their articulation to the democratic and social demands of the workers in the countries involved, deep study of the ongoing revolts in the countries of the South and of their limits and diverse possible evolutions, deep study of the struggles undertaken by the peoples of Europe and America—these constitute an inescapable precondition to carrying out fruitful discussion about possible futures.

It remains the case that any movement to break out from the internationalism deficit is far from visible. Is the second wave of struggles to transform the world, then, to be a remake of the first? In regard to Europe, the object of our present reflections, the anti-imperialist dimension remains absent from the consciousness of the actors in the struggle and from the strategies they develop—if they have strategies at all. I insist on concluding my reflections on "Europe seen from outside" with this remark, which I consider of the highest importance.

5. THE SOCIALIST ALTERNATIVE: CHALLENGE FOR THE RADICAL LEFT

GLOBALIZED CAPITALISM, only yesterday having declared the end of history, did not survive more than two decades before imploding. But what other world is being called forth to succeed it? Will capitalism enter a new phase in its deployment, less unbalanced globally and more centered in Asia and South America? Or will we see a truly polycentric world in which various popular democratic alternatives that arise are confronted by violent measures of capitalist restoration? The way to shed light on the nature of the ongoing systemic crisis is to return to a reading of the historical trajectory of capitalism. Such a debate opens the way for the radical left movements, if they can be bold, be major catalyzing forces for change, capable of advancing the emancipation of workers and peoples.

The Trajectory of Historical Capitalism

The long history of capitalism is composed of three distinct, successive phases: (1) a lengthy preparation—the transition from the tributary mode, the usual form of organization of premodern societies—which lasted eight centuries, from 1000 to 1800; (2) a short period of maturity (the nineteenth century), during which the "West" affirmed its domination; (3) the long "decline" caused by the "awakening of the South" (to use the title of my book, published by Le Temps des Cerises, Paris, in 2007) in which the peoples and their states regained the major initiative in transforming the world, the first wave having taken place in the twentieth century. This struggle against the imperialist order, inseparable from the global expansion of capitalism, is itself the potential agent in a commitment to the long road of transition, beyond capitalism, toward socialism. In the twenty-first century, there are the beginnings of a second wave of independent initiatives by the peoples and states of the South.

The internal contradictions that were characteristic of all the advanced societies in the premodern world, and not only those specific to "feudal" Europe, account for the successive waves of the inventions that were to constitute capitalist modernity.

The oldest wave came from China, where changes began in the Sung era (eleventh century), which developed further in the Ming and Qing epochs, giving China a head start in terms of technological inventiveness and the social productivity of collective work, which was not to be surpassed by Europe until the nineteenth century. This "Chinese" wave was to be followed by a "Middle Eastern" wave, which took place in the Arabo-Persian Caliphate and then (with the Crusades) in the towns of Italy.

The last wave concerns the long transition of the ancient tributary world to the modern capitalist world, which began in the Atlantic part of Europe as from the conquest of the Americas, and took the form of mercantilism for three centuries (1500–1800). Capitalism, which gradually came to dominate the world, is the result of this last wave. The European/"Western" form of historical capitalism that took place in Atlantic and Central Europe, with offspring in the United States and, later on, in Japan, developed its own characteristics, particularly its accumulation mode based on dispossession, first of the peasants and then of the peoples in the peripheries, integrated into its global system. This historical form is therefore indissoluble from the centers/peripheries contrast that it endlessly constructs, reproduces, and deepens.

Historical capitalism took on its final form at the end of the eighteenth century with the English Industrial Revolution that invented the new "machine factory" (together with the creation of the new industrial proletariat) and the French Revolution that invented modern politics.

Mature capitalism developed over the short period that marked the apogee of this system in the nineteenth century. Capital accumulation then took on its definitive form and became the basic law that governed society.

From the beginning, this form of accumulation was constructive (it enabled a prodigious and continuous acceleration in the productivity of social labor), but it was, at the same time, destructive. Marx observed that at an early stage accumulation destroys the two bases of wealth: the human being (victim of commodity alienation) and nature.

In my analyses of historical capitalism, I particularly stressed the third aspect of this destructive dimension of accumulation: the material and cultural dispossession of the dominated peoples of the periphery, which Marx had perhaps somewhat overlooked. This was no doubt because in the short period when Marx was producing his works, Europe seemed almost exclusively dedicated to the requirements of internal accumulation. He thus relegated this dispossession to a phase of "primitive accumulation," which I, on the contrary, have described as permanent.

The fact remains that during its short mature period, capitalism fulfilled undeniable progressive functions. It created the conditions that made it possible and necessary for it to be overtaken by socialism/communism, both on the material level and on that of the new political and cultural consciousness that accompanied it. Socialism (and even more so, communism) is not a superior "mode of production" because it is capable of accelerating the development of the forces of production and to associating them with an "equitable" distribution of income. It is something else again: a higher stage in the development of human civilization. It is not therefore by chance that the worker and socialist movement began to take root in the new popular classes and was committed to the fight for socialism as from the European nineteenth century (with the *Communist Manifesto*, as from 1848). Nor is it by chance that this challenge took the form of the first socialist revolution in history: the Paris Commune in 1871.

As from the end of the nineteenth century, capitalism entered into its long period of decline. I mean by this that the destructive dimensions of accumulation now won out, at a growing rate, over its progressive, constructive dimension.

This qualitative transformation of capitalism took shape with the setting up of new production monopolies (and no longer only in the areas of trade and colonial conquest as in the mercantilist period) at the end of the nineteenth century (described by Hobson, Hilferding, Lenin) in response to the first long structural crisis of capitalism that started in the

1870s (shortly after the defeat of the Paris Commune). The emergence of monopoly capitalism showed that capitalism had by now "had its day," that it had become "obsolete." The bell sounded for the necessary and possible expropriation of the expropriators. This decline found its expression in the first wave of wars and revolutions that marked the history of the twentieth century.

Lenin was therefore right in describing monopoly capitalism as the "highest stage of capitalism." But, optimistically, he thought that this first long crisis would be the last, with the socialist revolution getting on the agenda. History later proved that capitalism was able to overcome this crisis (at the cost of two world wars and by adapting to the setbacks imposed on it by the Russian and Chinese socialist revolutions and national liberation in Asia and Africa). But after the short period of monopoly capitalism's revival (1945–1975), there followed a second, long structural crisis of the system, starting in the 1970s. Capital reacted to this renewed challenge by a qualitatively new transformation that took the form of what I have described as "generalized monopoly capitalism."

A host of major questions arise from this interpretation of the "long decline" of capitalism, which concern the nature of the "revolution" that was the order of the day. Could the "long decline" of historical monopoly capitalism be synonymous with the "long transition" to socialism/communism? Under what conditions?

I see the history of this long transition of capitalism as the process of invention of the ingredients, which, when brought together, constitute historical capitalism in its final form. These ingredients include the social relations—and especially property relations—of capitalism, in other words, the polarization between the exclusive owners of the modern means of production (the factory) and the labor force, which has been reduced to commodity status. Of course, because the emergence of these relations defines capitalism, the confusion between "commerce" and "capitalism" has extremely weakened the understanding of the reality of the modern world. This Eurocentric reading of Marxism reduces the long transition to capitalism to the three centuries of European mercantilism. Moreover, the Eurocentric framework reinforces the tendency to confuse merchant capitalism with capitalism itself, so much so that the qualitative transformation represented by the Industrial Revolution, the invention of machine manufacturing, is even sometimes called into question.

The understanding of history is further narrowed from the perspectives of Eurocentrism to those of Anglocentrism, in which the moment of European transition is reduced to that of a particular form of transformation of English agriculture. With "enclosures" the peasant majority was expropriated and access to land restricted to aristocratic landlords and the rich peasants who were their tenant farmers. In fact, other forms of industrial capitalism also emerged linked with other forms of capitalist management of agriculture in the United States, France and the European continent, Japan, and elsewhere.

The historical reading I propose is non-Eurocentric not simply because it includes contributions from other regions of the world to the invention of capitalism. It stems from a non-reductionist reading of the concept of the mode of production. Capitalism is more than a mode of production at a more advanced stage of the development of productive forces; it is a more advanced stage of civilization. And for this reason, the invention of the social relations of capitalism is inseparable from that of other elements of what became "modernity."

The creation of a public service recruited by competitive examination, the idea of a secular state, the conviction that humans—not gods or aristocratic ancestors—make history, started in China centuries before Europe, and all constituted ingredients of *capitalist modernity*. Modernity as we know it is capitalist modernity, defined by the contradictions inherent in the hegemony of capital and the limitations that therefore ensue.

I have, moreover, proposed an understanding of the capitalist mode of production that, taking into consideration all the levels of its reality (the "instances" in Marxian writings), linking its economic base and its political and ideological superstructures, accounts for the autonomy of the specific logic of deployment of each of these levels or "instances" of reality.

I would also say that mercantile capitalism at an advanced stage of development—in China, the Muslim Caliphate, in the Italian city-states, and finally in European mercantilism—acquired a new meaning: it is understood as the precursor of the advanced capitalism brought about by the Industrial Revolution. Even if mercantile capitalism was for a long time captive of the social relations that defined the tributary mode of production, in other words remained "embedded" (to use Polanyi's phrase) in a system that was defined by the dominance of the political "instance" and submission of the economy to the requirements of its reproduction, the fact remains that the eventual development of capitalism depended upon essential elements of mercantilism, such as sophisticated forms of accounting and credit.

From 1500 (the beginning of the Atlantic mercantilist form of the transition to mature capitalism) to 1900 (the beginning of the challenge to the unilateral logic of accumulation), the Westerners (Europeans, then North Americans, and later, the Japanese) remained the masters of the game. They alone shaped the structures of the new world of historical capitalism. The peoples and nations of the periphery that had been conquered and dominated did, of course, resist as they could, but they were always finally defeated and forced to adapt to their subordinate status.

The domination of the Euro-Atlantic world was accompanied by its demographic explosion: the Europeans, who had constituted 18 percent of the planet's population in 1500, represented 36 percent by 1900, increased by their descendants emigrating to the Americas and Australia. Without this massive emigration, the accumulation model of historical capitalism, based on the accelerated disappearance of the peasant world, would simply have been impossible. This is why the model cannot be reproduced in the peripheries of the system, which have no "Americas" to conquer. "Catching up" in the system being impossible, they have no alternative to opting for a different development path.

The twentieth century saw the beginning of a reversal of the roles: the initiative passed to the peoples and nations of the periphery.

In 1871, the Paris Commune, which, as mentioned, was the first socialist revolution, also proved to be the last one to take place in a country in the capitalist center. The twentieth century inaugurated, with the "awakening of the peoples of the peripheries," a new chapter in history, its first manifestations being the revolution in Iran of 1907, in Mexico (1910–1920), in China (1911), in "semi-periphery" Russia in 1905, heralding 1917, the Arabo-Muslim Nahda, the constitution of the Young Turk movement, the Egyptian revolution of 1919, the formation of the Indian Congress.

In reaction to the first long crisis of historical capitalism (1875–1950), the peoples of the periphery began to liberate themselves as from 1914–1917, mobilizing themselves under the flags of socialism (Russia, China, Vietnam, Cuba) or of national liberation, associated to different degrees with progressive social reforms. They took the path to industrialization, hitherto forbidden by the domination of the (old) "classic" imperialism, forcing the latter to "adjust" to this first wave of independent initiatives of the peoples, nations, and states of the peripheries. From 1917 to the time when the Bandung Project (1955–1980) ran out of steam and the collapse of Sovietism in 1990, these were the initiatives that dominated the scene.

I do not see the two long crises of aging monopoly capitalism in terms of the long Kondratieff cycles, but as two stages in the decline of historical globalized capitalism and the possible transition to socialism. Nor do I see the 1914–45 period exclusively as "the thirty years' war for the succession to British hegemony," but as the long war being conducted by the imperialist centers against the first awakening of the peripheries (East and South).

This first wave of the awakening of the peoples of the periphery wore out for many reasons, due both to its own internal limitations and contradictions and to the success of imperialism in finding new ways of dominating the world system—through the control of technological invention, access to resources, the globalized financial system, communication and information technology, weapons of mass destruction.

Nevertheless, capitalism underwent a second long crisis that began in the 1970s, exactly one hundred years after the first one. The reactions of capital to this crisis were the same as to the previous one: reinforced concentration (which gave rise to generalized monopoly capitalism), globalization, and financialization. But the moment of triumph of the new collective imperialism of the Triad—the United States, Europe, and Japan—(the second "belle époque," from 1990 to 2008, echoing the first belle époque, 1890–1914) was indeed brief. A new epoch of chaos, wars, and revolutions emerged. In this situation, the second wave of the awakening of the nations of the periphery (which had already started), now refuses to allow the collective imperialism of the Triad to maintain its dominant positions other than through the military control of the planet. The Washington establishment, by giving priority to this strategic objective, proves that it is perfectly aware of the real issues at stake in the struggles and decisive conflicts of our epoch, as opposed to the naïve vision of the majority currents in Western *alterworldism*.

Is Generalized-Monopoly Capitalism the Last Phase of Capitalism?

Lenin had described the imperialism of the monopolies as the "highest stage of capitalism." I described imperialism as a "permanent phase of capitalism" in the sense that globalized historical capitalism has built up and never ceases from reproducing and deepening the center/periphery polarization. The first wave of monopolization at the end of the nineteenth century certainly involved a qualitative transformation in the fundamental structures of the capitalist mode of production. Lenin deduced from this that the socialist revolution was thus on the agenda and Rosa Luxemburg believed that the alternative was now in terms of "socialism or barbarism." Lenin was certainly rather too optimistic, having underestimated the devastating effects of the imperialist rent, and the associated transfer of the revolution from the West (the centers) to the East (the peripheries).

The second wave of the centralization of capital, which took place in the last third of the twentieth century, constituted a second qualitative transformation of the system, which I have described as generalized monopolies. From now on they not only commanded the heights of the modern economy; they succeeded in imposing their direct control over the whole production system. The small and medium enterprises (and even the large ones outside the monopolies), like the farmers, were literally dispossessed, reduced to the status of subcontractors, with their upstream and downstream operations subjected to rigid control by the monopolies.

At this highest phase of the centralization of capital, its ties with a living organic body—the bourgeoisie—have broken. This is an immensely important change: the historical bourgeoisie, constituted of families rooted locally, has given way to an anonymous oligarchy/plutocracy that controls the monopolies, in spite of the dispersion of the title deeds of their capital. The range of financial operations invented over the last decades bears witness to this supreme form of alienation: the speculator can now sell what he does not even possess, so that the principle of property is reduced to a status that is little less than derisory.

The function of socially productive labor has disappeared. The high degree of alienation had already attributed a productive virtue to money— "money makes little ones." Now alienation has reached new heights: it is time (time is money) that by its virtue alone "produces profit." The new bourgeois class that responds to the requirements of the reproduction of the system has been reduced to the status of "waged servants" (precarious, to boot), even when they are, as members of the upper sectors of the middle classes, privileged people who are very well paid for their "work."

This being so, should one not conclude that capitalism has had its day? There is no other possible answer to the challenge: the monopolies must be nationalized. This is a first, unavoidable step toward a possible socialization of their management by workers and citizens. Only this will make it possible to make progress along the long road to socialism. At the same time it will be the only way to develop a new macro economy that restores a genuine space for the operations of small and medium enterprises. If that is not done, the logic of domination by abstract capital can produce nothing but the decline of democracy and civilization, and a "generalized apartheid" at the world level.

Marxism's Tricontinental Vocation

My interpretation of historical capitalism stresses the polarization of the world (the contrast of center/periphery) produced by the historical form of the accumulation of capital. This questions the visions of the socialist revolution (and, more broadly the transition to socialism) that the historical Marxisms have developed. The "revolution" (or the transition) before us is not necessarily the one on which these visions have been based, nor are the strategies for fighting to overcome capitalism.

It has to be recognized that the most important social and political struggles of the twentieth century challenged not so much capitalism in itself as the permanent imperialist dimension of really existing capitalism. The question is therefore to know whether this transfer of the center of gravity of the struggles necessarily (still less automatically) calls capitalism into question, at least potentially. "Marxism" or, more exactly, historical Marxisms, were confronted by a new challenge, which did not exist in the most lucid political consciousness of the nineteenth century, but arose because of the transfer of the initiative to transform the world to the peoples, nations, and states of the periphery.

Imperialist rent not only benefited the monopolies of the dominant center (in the form of super-profits), it was also the basis of the reproduction of society as a whole, in spite of its evident class structure and the exploitation of its workers. "Another world" (a vague phrase to indicate a world committed to the long road toward socialism) is obviously impossible unless it provides a solution to the problems of the peoples in the periphery (only 80 percent of the world population). "Changing the world" therefore means changing the living conditions of this majority. Marxism, which analyzes the reality of the world to make the forces acting for change as effective as possible, necessarily acquires a decisive tricontinental (Africa, Asia, Latin America) vocation, if not a dominant one. So, how does it propose analyzing the reality and formulating effective action strategies?

The response to this question must be based on an analysis of the reality. What I propose is an analysis of what I consider to be the transformation of imperialist monopoly capitalism (senile) to generalized monopoly capitalism (still more senile for this reason). This is a qualitative transformation in response to the second long crisis of the system that began in the 1970s and has still not been solved. From this analysis I draw two main conclusions: 1) the transformation of the imperialist system into the collective imperialism of the Triad in reaction to the industrialization of the peripheries, imposed by the victories of the first wave of their "awakening," together with the implementation by the new imperialism of new means of control of the world system, based on the military control of the planet and its resources, the super-protection of the exclusive appropriation of technology by the oligopolies, and their control over the world financial system; and 2) the transformation of the class structures of contemporary capitalism that has developed with the emergence of an exclusive dominant oligarchy.

In contrast, Mao developed a reflection that was both profoundly revolutionary and "realistic" (scientific, lucid) about the terms in which the challenge should be analyzed, making it possible to deduct effective strategies for successive advances along the long road of transition to socialism. For this reason, he distinguishes and connects the three *dimensions* of reality: peoples, nations, states.

The people (popular classes) "want the revolution." This means that it is possible to construct a hegemonic coalition that brings together the different dominated and exploited classes as opposed to the one that enables the reproduction of the system of the domination of imperialist capitalism, exercised through the comprador hegemonic coalition and the state at its service.

The mention of nations refers to the fact that imperialist domination denies the dignity of the "nations" (call them what you will), forged by the history of the societies of the peripheries. Such domination has systematically destroyed all that gives the nations their originality, to the profit of Westernization's cheap junk. The liberation of the people is therefore inseparable from that of the nations to which they belong. And this is the reason why Maoism replaced the short slogan "Workers of all countries, unite!" by a more embracing one, "Workers of all countries, oppressed peoples, unite!" Nations want their liberation, seen as being complementary to the struggle of the people and not in conflict with it. The liberation in question is not therefore the restoration of the past—the illusion of a culturalist attachment to the past—but the invention of the future based on the radical transformation of their historical heritage, rather than the artificial importation of a false "modernity." The culture that is inherited and subjected to the test of transformation is understood here as the political culture, care being taken not to use the vague term "culture" (religion and other aspects of culture), which does not mean anything because it is not a historical invariant.

The reference to the state is based on the necessary recognition of the autonomy of its power in relation to the hegemonic coalition that is the base of its legitimacy, even if this is popular and national. This autonomy cannot be ignored as long as the state exists, that is, at least for the whole duration of the transition to communism. It is only after this that we can think of a "stateless society," not before. Not only because the popular and national advances must be protected from the permanent aggression of imperialism, which still dominates the world, but also, and perhaps above all, because "to advance on the long transition" also requires "developing productive forces." In other words, to achieve that which imperialism has been preventing in the countries in the periphery and to obliterate the heritage of world polarization, which is inseparable from the world expansion of historical capitalism. The program is not the same as "catching up" through imitation of the centers' capitalism—a catching up that is, incidentally, impossible and above all, undesirable. It imposes a different conception of "modernization/industrialization" based on the genuine participation of the popular classes in the process of implementation, with immediate benefits for them at each stage as it advances. We must therefore reject the dominant reasoning that demands people to wait indefinitely until the development of the productive forces has finally created the conditions of a "necessary" passage to socialism. These must be developed right from the beginning with the prospect of constructing socialism. The power of the state is evidently at the heart of the conflicts between these contradictory requirements of "development" and "socialism."

"The states want independence." This must be seen as a twofold objective: independence (extreme form of autonomy) vis-à-vis the popular classes, independence from the pressures of the capitalist world system. The "bourgeoisie" (broadly speaking, the governing class in commanding positions of the state, whose ambitions always tend toward a bourgeois evolution) is both national and comprador. If circumstances enable them to increase their autonomy vis-à-vis dominant imperialism, they choose to "defend the national interest." But if circumstances do not so permit, they will opt for comprador submission to the requirements of imperialism. The "new governing class" (or "governing group") is still in an ambiguous position, even when it is based on a popular coalition, by the fact that it is animated by a "bourgeois" tendency, at least partially.

The correct articulation of reality at these three levels conditions the success of the progress on the long road of the transition. It is a question of reinforcing the complementarity of the advances of the people, the liberation of the nation, and achievements by the power of the state. But if contradictions between the popular agent and the state agent are allowed to develop, any advances are finally doomed. There will be an impasse if one of these levels is not concerned about its articulation with the others. The notion of the "people" as being the only ones that count—the thesis of the "movement," which is that they are capable of transforming the world without worrying about taking over power—is simply naïve. Whereas the notion of national liberation "at all costs," in other words being independent of the social content of the hegemonic coalition, leads to the cultural illusion of attachment to the past (political Islam, Hinduism, and Buddhism are examples) is in fact powerless.

The notion of power, conceived as being capable of "achievements" for the people, but carried out without them, leads to the drift to authoritarianism and the crystallization of a new bourgeoisie. The deviation of

Sovietism, evolving from "capitalism without capitalists" (state capitalism) to "capitalism with capitalists," is the most tragic example of this.

As peoples, nations, and states of the periphery do not accept the imperialist system, the "South" is the "storm zone," one of permanent uprisings and revolts. And since 1917, history has consisted mainly of these revolts and independent initiatives (in the sense of independence of the tendencies that dominate the existing imperialist capitalist system) of the peoples, nations, and states of the peripheries. It is these initiatives, despite their limits and contradictions, that have shaped the most decisive transformations of the contemporary world, far more than the progress of the productive forces and the relatively easy social adjustments that accompanied them in the heartlands of the system.

The second wave of independent initiatives of the countries of the South has begun. The "emerging" countries and others, like their peoples, are fighting the ways in which the collective imperialism of the Triad tries to perpetuate its domination. The military interventions of Washington and their subaltern NATO allies have also proved a failure. The world financial system is collapsing and in its place autonomous regional systems are in the process of being set up. The technological monopoly of the oligopolies has been thwarted. Recovering control over natural resources is now the order of the day. The Andean nations, victims of the internal colonialism that succeeded foreign colonization, are making themselves felt on the political stage. The popular organizations and the parties of the radical left in struggle have already defeated some liberal programs (in Latin America) or are on the way to doing so. These initiatives, which are first of all fundamentally anti-imperialist, are potentially able to commit themselves along the long road to the socialist transition.

How do these two possible futures relate to each other? The "other world" that is being built is always ambivalent: it carries the worst and the best within it, both of them "possible" (there are no laws in history previous to history itself to give us an indication, as I have said). A first wave of initiatives by the peoples, nations, and states of the periphery took place in the twentieth century, until 1980. Any analysis of its components makes no sense unless thought is given to the complementarities and conflicts on how the three levels relate to each other. A second wave of initiatives has already started. Will it be more effective? Can it go further than the preceding one?

Ending the Crisis of Capitalism?

The oligarchies in power of the contemporary capitalist system are trying to restore the system as it was before the financial crisis of 2008. For this they need to convince people through a "consensus" that does not challenge their supreme power. To succeed in this they are prepared to make some rhetorical concessions about the ecological challenges (in particular about the question of the climate), green-washing their domination and even hinting that they will carry out social reforms (the "war on poverty") and political reforms ("good governance").

To take part in this game and the effort of convincing people that a consensus—even defined in terms that are clearly better—will end up in failure and, worse still, it will prolong fatal illusions. This is because the response to the challenge first requires the transformation of power relationships to the benefit of the workers as well as of international relationships to the benefit of the peoples of the peripheries. The United Nations has organized a whole series of global conferences, which have yielded nothing, as one might have expected.

History has proved that this is a necessary requirement. The response to the first long crisis of aging capitalism took place between 1914 and 1950, mainly through the conflicts that opposed the peoples of the peripheries to the domination of the imperial powers and, to different degrees, through the internal social relationships benefiting the popular classes. In this way they prepared the path for the three systems of the post–Second World War period: the really existing socialisms of that time, the national and popular regimes of Bandung, the social-democrat compromise in the countries of the North, which had been made particularly necessary by the advances started by the independent initiatives of the peoples of the peripheries.

In 2008 the second long crisis of capitalism moved into a new phase. Violent international conflicts have already begun and are visible: would they challenge the domination of the generalized monopolies, based on anti-imperialist positions? How do they relate to the social struggles of the victims of the austerity policies pursued by the dominant classes in response to the crisis? In other words, will the peoples replace a strategy of extricating themselves from a capitalism in crisis, instead of the strategy to extricate the system from its crisis, as pursued by the powers that be?

The ideologues serving power are running out of steam, making futile remarks about the "world after the crisis." The CIA can only envisage a restoration of the system, attributing greater participation to the "emerging markets" in the liberal globalization, to the detriment of Europe, rather than of the United States. It never contemplates that the crisis, which will increase and deepen, will not be overcome, except through violent international and social conflict. No one knows how it will turn out: it could be for the better (progress in the direction of socialism) or for the worse (world apartheid).

The political radicalization of the social struggles is the condition for overcoming their fragmentation and their exclusively defensive strategy— "safeguarding social benefits." Only this will make it possible to identify the objectives needed for undertaking the long road to socialism. Only this will enable the "movements" to gain real power—the English term "empowerment" is the best way of expressing what is needed.

The empowerment of the movements requires a framework of macro political and economic conditions that make their concrete projects viable. How to create these conditions? Here we come to the central question of the power of the state. But would a renewed state, genuinely popular and democratic, be capable of carrying out effective policies in the globalization conditions of the contemporary world? A rapid, negative reply has then called for prior research to achieve a minimal global consensus. This response and its corollary are proving fruitless. There is no other solution than advances made at the national level, perhaps reinforced by appropriate action at the regional level. They must aim at dismantling the world system (the de-linking) before eventual reconstruction, on a different basis, with the prospect of overtaking capitalism. The principle is as valid for the countries of the South which, incidentally, have started to move in this direction in Asia and Latin America, as it is for the countries of the North where, alas, need for the dismantling the European institutions (and that of the euro) is not yet envisaged, even by the radical left.

The Indispensable Internationalism of the Workers and the Peoples

The limits of the advances made by the awakening of the South in the twentieth century and the exacerbation of the contradictions that resulted was the cause of the first liberation wave losing its impetus. And it was greatly reinforced by the permanent hostility of the states in the imperialist center, which went to the extent of waging open warfare that, it has to be said, was supported—or at least accepted—by the peoples of the North. The benefits of the imperialist rent were certainly an important factor in this rejection of internationalism by the peoples of the North. The communist minorities, who adopted another attitude, sometimes strongly so, nevertheless failed to build effective alternative coalitions around themselves. And the passing of the socialist parties en masse into the "anti-communist" camp largely contributed to the success of the capitalist powers in the imperialist camp. These parties have not, however, been "rewarded," as the very day after the collapse of the first wave of struggles of the twentieth century, monopoly capitalism shook off their alliance. These parties have not learned the lesson of their defeat by radicalizing themselves: on the contrary they have chosen to capitulate by sliding into the "social-liberal" positions with which we are familiar. This is the proof, if such was needed, of the decisive role of the imperialist rent in the reproduction of the societies in the North. Thus the second capitulation was not so much a tragedy as a farce.

The defeat of internationalism shares part of the responsibility for the authoritarian drifts toward autocracy in the socialist experiences of the past century. The explosion of inventive expressions of democracy during the course of the Russian and Chinese revolutions gives the lie to the too easy judgment, according to which the societies of these countries were not "ripe" for democracy. The hostility of the imperialist countries, facilitated by the support of their peoples, largely contributed in making the pursuit of democratic socialist progress even harder in conditions that were already difficult, created by the inheritance of peripheral capitalism.

Thus the second wave of the awakening of the peoples, nations, and states of the peripheries of the twenty-first century starts out in conditions that are barely better, in fact even more difficult. The U.S. ideologues of the "consensus" (meaning submission to the requirements of the power of the generalized-monopoly capitalism), the adoption of "presidential" political regimes that destroy the effectiveness of the anti-establishment potential of democracy, the indiscriminate eulogy of a false, manipulated individualism, together with inequality, the rallying of the subaltern NATO countries to the strategies implemented by the Washington establishment—all these are making rapid headway in the European Union that cannot be, in these conditions, anything other than what it is: a constitutive coalition of imperialist globalization.

In this situation, the collapse of this military project becomes the first priority and the preliminary condition for the success of the second wave of the liberation being undertaken through the struggles of the peoples, nations, and states of the three continents. Until this happens, their present and future advances will remain vulnerable. A possible remake of the twentieth century is not therefore to be excluded even if, obviously, the conditions of our epoch are quite different from those of the last century.

This tragic scenario is not the only possible one, however. The offensive of capital against the workers is already under way in the very heartlands of the system. This is a proof, if it were necessary, that capital, when it is reinforced by its victories against the peoples of the periphery, is then able to frontally attack the positions of the working classes in the centers of the system. In this situation, it is no longer impossible to visualize the radicalization of the struggles. The heritage of European political cultures is not yet lost and should facilitate the rebirth of an international consciousness that meets the requirements of its globalization. An evolution in this direction, however, comes up against the obstacle of the imperialist rent. This is not only a major source of exceptional profits for the monopolies, it also conditions the reproduction of the society as a whole. And with the support of the people concerned for the existing electoral model of democracy, the weight of the middle classes can destroy the potential strength of the radicalization of the popular classes. Because of this, it is most likely that the progress in the tricontinental South will continue to be at the forefront of the scene, as in the last century. Yet as soon as the advances have had their effects and seriously restricted the extent of the imperialist rent, the peoples of the North should be in a better position to understand the failure of strategies that submit to the requirements of the generalized imperialist monopolies. The ideological and political forces of the radical left should take their place in this great movement of liberation built on the solidarity of peoples and workers.

The ideological and cultural battle is decisive for this renaissance, which I summarize in the strategic objective of building up a Fifth International of workers and peoples.

The Challenge for the South: A Shift in the Center of Gravity of Global Capitalism?

Do the victories of the anti-imperialist struggles of the states and peoples of the peripheries prepare the way for socialism or for the building of new centers of capitalism?

The present conjuncture seems to indicate an opposition between the decline of the old centers of the capitalist Triad in crisis, with the surge in capitalism in the growth of emerging countries (China and others). Would the current crisis then not lead to a new rise of capitalism, now centered in Asia and South America? This would mean that the victories of the anti-imperialist struggles of emerging countries would lead not to socialism but to a new rise of capitalism, albeit less polarized than it was before.

The main argument of my critique of this popular thesis proceeds from the observation that the pattern of historical capitalism, now promoted as the only option, depended from the beginning (European mercantilism) on the production and reproduction of global polarization. This feature is itself the product of the mass expulsion of the peasantry on which the development of capitalism was founded. The model was sustainable only through the safety valve allowed by the mass emigration to the Americas. It would be absolutely impossible for the countries of the periphery today— who make up 80 percent of the world's people, of which almost half are rural—to reproduce this model. They would need five or six Americas to be able to "catch up" in the same way. Catching up is therefore an illusion and any progress in this direction can only result in an impasse. This is why I say that the anti-imperialist struggles are potentially anti-capitalist. If we cannot "catch up," we might as well "do something else."

Of course, such a transformation in the long-term visions of emerging countries for "development" is by no means "inescapable." It is only necessary and possible. The current success of emerging countries in terms of accelerated growth within globalized capitalism and with capitalist means reinforces the illusion that catching up is possible. The same illusion accompanied the experiences of the first wave of "the awakening of the South" in the twentieth century, even though at that time they were experienced as a "catch-up by the road of socialism." I analyzed the contradictions of the Bandung Project (1955–1980) in the same terms, given the conflicting projects of the national bourgeoisies and working classes allied in the struggles for liberation.

Today the collective imperialism of the Triad makes use of all the means at its disposal—economic, financial, and military—to continue its domination of the world. Emerging countries that take on strategies to eliminate the advantages of the Triad—the control of technologies, control of access to the globe's natural resources, and the military control of the planet—are therefore in conflict with the Triad. This conflict helps to dispel any illusions about their ability "to advance within the system" and gives popular democratic forces the possibility of influencing the course of events in the direction of progress on the long road of the transition to socialism.

Three Major Challenges: Democracy, the Agrarian Question, the Environment

"Democracy" or Democratization Associated with Social Progress

It was a stroke of genius of Atlantic alliance diplomacy to choose the field of "democracy" for their offensive, which was aimed, from the beginning, at the dismantling of the Soviet Union and the reconquest of the countries of Eastern Europe. This decision goes back to the 1970s and gradually became crystallized in the Conference of the Organization for Security and Cooperation in Europe (OSCE) and then with the signing of the Helsinki Final Act in 1975. Jacques Andreani, in his book with the evocative title *Le Piège, Helsinki et la chute du communisme* (The Trap: Helsinki and the Fall of Communism), explains how the Soviets, who were expecting an agreement on the disarmament of NATO and a genuine détente, were quite simply deceived by their Western partners. It was a stroke of genius because the "question of democracy" was a genuine issue and the least one could say was that the Soviet regimes were certainly not "democratic," however one defined its concept and practice. The countries of the Atlantic alliance, in contrast, could qualify themselves as "democratic," whatever the limitations and contradictions in their actual political practices, subordinated to the requirements of capitalist reproduction. The comparison of the systems operated in their favor.

This discourse on democracy was then gradually replaced by the one supported by the Soviets and their allies: "pacific coexistence," associated with "respect" for the political practices of both parties and for "non-interference" in their internal affairs. The coexistence discourse had had its important moments. For example, the Stockholm Appeal in the 1950s, reminded people of the real nuclear threat implied by the aggressive diplomacy employed by the United States since the Potsdam Conference (1945), reinforced by the atomic bombing of Japan just a few days after the conference.

However, at the same time the choice of this strategy (coexistence and non-interference) was convenient—or could be convenient, according to circumstances—to the dominant powers in both West and East. For it enabled the realities of the respective descriptions "capitalist" and "socialist" to be taken for granted by the countries of both West and East. It eliminated all serious discussion about the precise nature of the two systems: that is, from examining the actually existing capitalism of our era (oligopoly capitalism) and actually existing socialism. The United Nations (with the tacit agreement of the powers of the two worlds) changed the terms of "capitalism" and "socialism" to the "market economies" and the "centrally planned economies"—or, to be mischievous, the "administered economies."

These two terms, both of them false (or only superficially true), sometimes made it possible to emphasize the "convergence of the systems": a convergence that was itself imposed by modern technology (a theory, also false, derived from a monistic, technicist concept of history). It also accepted coexistence in order to facilitate this "natural" convergence or, on the contrary, stressed the irreducible opposition between the "democratic" model (associated with the market economy) and "totalitarianism" (produced by the administered economy), at certain moments during the cold war.

Choosing to concentrate the battle around the "democracy" discourse made it possible to opt for the "implacability" of systems and to offer the eastern countries only the prospect of capitulation by returning to capitalism (the market), which should then produce, naturally, the conditions for democratization. The fact that this has not been the case (for post-Soviet Russia), or has taken place in highly caricatural forms (for ethnic groups here and there in Eastern Europe) is another matter.

The "democratic" discourse of the countries of the Atlantic alliance is recent. At the outset NATO accommodated itself perfectly well to Salazar in Portugal, the Turkish generals, and the Greek colonels. At the same time the Triad diplomacies supported (and often established) the worst dictatorships that Latin America, Africa, and Asia had ever known. At first the new democratic discourse was adopted with much reticence. Many of the main political authorities of the Atlantic alliance saw the inconveniences that could upset their preferred realpolitik. It was not until Carter was president of the United States (rather like Obama today) that the "moral" sermon conveyed by democracy was understood. It was Mitterrand in France who broke with the Gaullist tradition of refusing the "division" imposed on Europe by the cold war strategy promoted by the United States. Later, the experience of Gorbachev in the USSR made it clear that rallying to this discourse was a guarantee for catastrophe.

The new "democratic" discourse thus bore its fruits. It seemed sufficiently convincing for "left-wing" opinion in Europe to support it. This was so, not only for the electoral left (the socialist parties) but also those with a more radical tradition, of which the Communist parties were the heir. With "eurocommunism" the consensus became general.

The dominant classes of the imperialist Triad learned lessons from their victory. They thus decided to continue this strategy of centering the debate on the "democratic question." China is not reproached for having opened up its economy to the outside world, but because its policies are managed by the Communist Party. No account is taken of the social achievements of Cuba, unequalled in the whole of Latin America, but its one-party system is constantly stigmatized. The same discourse is even leveled against Putin's Russia.

Is the triumph of democracy the real objective of this strategy? One has to be very naïve to think so. The only aim is to impose on recalcitrant countries the "market economy," open and integrated into the so-called liberal world system. This is in reality imperialistic, its purpose being to reduce these countries to the status of dominated peripheries of the system. This is an objective that, once achieved, becomes an obstacle to the progress of democracy in the victimized countries and is in no way an advance in response to the "democratic question." The chances of democratic progress in the countries that practiced "actually existing socialism" (at least at the beginning) would have been much greater, in the medium term if not immediately. The dialectics of social struggles would have been left to develop on their own, opening up the possibility of outstripping the limits of "actually existing socialism," which had, moreover, been deformed by at a partial adherence to the opening of the liberal economy, to reach the "end of the tunnel."

In actual fact the "democratic" theme is only invoked against countries that do not want to open up to the globalized liberal economy. There is less concern for highly autocratic political regimes. Saudi Arabia and Pakistan are good examples, but also Georgia (pro the Atlantic alliance) and many others. Besides, at the very best, the proposed "democratic" formula hardly goes beyond the caricature of "multiparty elections" that are not only completely alien to the requirements of social progress but are always, or almost always, associated with the social regression that the domination of actually existing capitalism (that of the oligopolies) demands and produces. The formula has already largely undermined democracy, for which many peoples, profoundly confused, have now substituted religious and ethnic attachment to the past.

It is therefore now more than ever necessary to reinforce the critique of the *radical* left (I emphasize radical to distinguish it from the critique of the left, which is confusing and vague). In other words it must be a critique that associates, rather than dissociates, the democratization of society (and not only its political management) with social progress (in a socialist perspective). In this critique, the struggle for democratization and the struggle for socialism are one and the same. No socialism without democracy, but also no democratic progress without a socialist perspective.

Democratization is an endless process, not to be reduced to pluriparty elected representative so-called democracy, which does not empower the people and permit them to transform society. Democratization is multidimensional. It integrates the major issue of gender as well as the guarantee of individual liberties, which should be developed, not restricted. It involves also collective social rights, with a view to socializing the management of the economy, moving therefore beyond capitalism, based on the sacred character of private property.

The New Agrarian Question:
Access to Land for All Peasants of the South

All societies before modern (capitalist) time were peasant societies, their production ruled by various specific systems and logics that were not those that rule capitalism (that is, the maximization of the return on capital in a market society).

Modern capitalist agriculture, represented by both rich family farming and/or by agribusiness corporations, is now looking forward to a massive attack on Third World peasant production. The project did get the green light from the WTO in its Doha session. The peasantry still makes up half of humankind, but its production is shared between two sectors enormously unequal in size with a clearly distinct economic and social character and levels of efficiency.

Capitalist agriculture governed by the principle of return on capital, which is localized almost exclusively in North America, in Europe, in the Southern Cone of Latin America, and in Australia, employs only a few tens of millions of farmers who are no longer "peasants." But their productivity, which depends on mechanization (of which they have monopoly worldwide) and the area of land possessed by each farmer, ranges between 10,000 and 20,000 quintals of equivalent cereals per worker annually.

On the other hand, peasant farming systems still constitute the occupation of nearly half of humanity—that is, three billion human beings. These farming systems are in turn shared between those who benefited from the green revolution (fertilizers, pesticides, and selected seeds), but are nevertheless poorly mechanized, with production ranging between 100 and 500 quintals per farmer, and the other group still excluded from this revolution, whose production is estimated around 10 quintals per farmer.

The new agrarian question is the result of that unequal development. Indeed, modernization had always combined constructive dimensions (accumulation of capital and progress of productivities) with destructive aspects (reducing labor to the stature of a commodity sold on the market, often destroying the natural ecological basis needed for the reproduction of life and production, polarizing wealth on a global level). Modernization had always simultaneously "integrated" those for whom employment was created by the expansion of markets, and "excluded" those who, having lost their positions in the previous systems, were not integrated into the new labor force. But, in its ascending phase, capitalist global expansion did integrate along with its excluding processes. But now, with respect to the area of Third World peasant societies, it would be massively excluding, including only insignificant minorities.

The question raised here is precisely whether this trend continues and will continue to operate with respect to the three billion human beings still producing and living in the frame of peasant societies, in Asia, Africa, and Latin America. Indeed, what would happen as of now should "agriculture and food production" be treated as any other form of production submitted to the rules of competition in an open-deregulated market as it has been decided in principle at the last WTO conference (Doha, November 2001)? Would such principles foster the accelerating of production?

Indeed, one can imagine some twenty million new additional modern farmers, producing whatever the three billion present peasants can offer on the market beyond ensuring their own (poor) self-subsistence. The conditions for the success of such an alternative would necessitate the transfer of important pieces of good land to the new agriculturalists (and these lands have to be taken out of the hands of present peasant societies), access to capital markets (to buy equipment) and access to the consumer markets. Such agriculturalists would indeed "compete" successfully with the billions of present peasants. But what would happen to those?

Under the circumstances, admitting the general principle of competition for agricultural products and foodstuffs, as imposed by WTO, means accepting that billions of "non-competitive" producers be eliminated within the short historic time of a few decades. What will become of these billions of human beings, the majority of whom are already poor among the poor, but who feed themselves with great difficulty, and worse still, what will be the plight of the one-third of this population (since three-quarters of the underfed population of the world are rural dwellers)? In fifty years' time, no relatively competitive industrial development, even in the fanciful hypothesis of a continued growth of 7 percent annually for three-quarters of humanity, could absorb even one-third of this reserve.

The major argument presented to legitimate the WTO-competition doctrine alternative is that such development did happen in nineteenth-century Europe and finally produced a modern-wealthy, urban-industrial post-industrial society as well as a modern agriculture able to feed the nations and even to export. Why should not this pattern be repeated in the contemporary Third World countries, in particular for the emerging nations?

The argument fails to consider two major factors that make the reproduction of the pattern almost impossible now in Third World countries. The first is that the European model developed throughout a century and a half along with industrial technologies that were labor-intensive. Modern technologies are far less so. And therefore if the newcomers of the Third World have to be competitive on global markets for their industrial exports they have to adopt them. The second is that Europe benefited during that long transition from the possibility of massive out-migration of their "surplus" population to the Americas.

That argument that capitalism has indeed "solved" the agrarian question in its developed centers has always been admitted by large sections of the left, including within historical Marxism, as testified by the famous book of Kautsky—*The Agrarian Question*—written before the First World War. Leninism itself inherited that view and on its basis undertook a modernization through the Stalinist collectivization, with dubious results. What was always overlooked was that capitalism, though it solved the question in its centers, did so through generating a gigantic agrarian question in the peripheries, which it cannot solve but through the genocide of half of humankind. Within historical Marxism only Maoism did understand the size of the challenge. Therefore those who charge Maoism with its "peasant deviation" show by this very criticism that they do not have the analytical capacity for an understanding of what is actually existing imperialist capitalism, which they reduce to an abstract discourse on capitalism in general.

Modernization through market liberalization as suggested by WTO and its supporters finally aligns side by side, without even necessarily combining two components: (1) the production of food on a global scale by modern competitive agriculturalists mostly based in the North but also possibly in the future in some pockets of the South; and (2) the marginalization—exclusion—and further impoverishment of the majority of the three billion peasants of the present Third World and finally their seclusion in some kinds of "reserves." It therefore combines (1) a pro-modernization, efficiency-dominant discourse; and (2) an ecological cultural reserve set of policies making it possible for the victims to "survive." These two components might therefore complement each other rather than conflict.

Can we imagine other alternatives and have them widely debated? In that frame it is implied that peasant agriculture should be maintained throughout the visible future of the twenty-first century but simultaneously engaged in a process of continuous technological/social change and progress. At a rate that would allow a progressive transfer to non-rural, non-agricultural employment. Such a strategic set of targets involves complex policy mixes at national, regional, and global levels.

At the national levels it implies macropolicies protecting peasant food production from the unequal competition of modernized agriculturalists—agro-business local and international. With a view to guaranteeing acceptable internal food prices eventually disconnected from the so-called international market prices (markets biased by subsidies of the wealthy Northern United States/Canada/Europe). Such policy targets also question the patterns of industrial–urban developments, which should be less based on export oriented priorities, themselves taking advantage of low wages (implying in their turn low prices for food), and be more attentive to a socially balanced internal market expansion.

A development strategy in keeping with the challenge must be based on the guarantee of access to land and to the means if its use to all peasants, as equally as possible. Yet the necessary progress of productivity of peasant family agriculture does need industries to support it. Industrialization therefore cannot be escaped from, but its patterns should not reproduce those of capitalism, which generates growing inequalities and ecological devastation. Programs that substitute for the inventing of new patterns of industrialization so-called foreign aid, associated with empty discourses (good governance, alleviating poverty) are nothing but the continuation of colonial discourses. The real objective of imperialism is to marginalize peoples. For imperialism African natural resources (oil, minerals, land) are important, not African peoples who represent rather an obstacle to the plunder of resources. Simultaneously such a choice of principle facilitates integrating in the overall scheme patterns of policies ensuring national food security, an indispensable condition for a country to be an active member of the global community, enjoying the indispensable margin of autonomy and negotiating capacity.

At regional and global levels it implies international agreements and policies moving away from the doctrinaire liberal principles ruling the WTO, imaginative and specific to different areas, since it has to take into consideration specific issues and concrete historical and social conditions.

The "Environment," or the Socialist Perspective of Use Value? The Ecological Question and So-Called Sustainable Development

Here, too, the point of departure is an acknowledgment of a real problem, the destruction of the natural environment and, at last resort, the survival of life on the planet, which has been brought about by the logic of capital accumulation. Here, too, the question dates back to the 1970s, more precisely the Stockholm Conference of 1972. But for a long time it was a minor issue, marginalized by all the dominant discourses and the practices of economic management. The question has only recently been put forward as a new central plank in the dominating strategy.

Taking into account use value (of which the ecological footprint constitutes the first good example) implies that socialism must be "ecological," cannot be anything but ecological. As Elmar Altvater has observed "solar socialism" or "no socialism." However, it also implies that it is impossible for any capitalist system whatsoever, even "reformed," to take it into account, as we shall see later.

In Marx's time, he not only suspected the existence of this problem, he had already formulated a rigorous distinction between value and wealth, which were confused by vulgar economics. He said explicitly that capitalist accumulation destroyed the natural bases on which it was founded: human beings (the alienated, exploited, dominated and oppressed worker) and the land (symbol of the natural wealth given to humanity). And whatever the limits of this expression, as always a prisoner of its epoch, it is nonetheless true that it shows a lucid awareness of the problem (beyond that of intuition), which should be recognized. It is therefore regrettable that the ecologists of our era have not read Marx (John Bellamy Foster is the brilliant exception). It would have enabled them to carry their propositions further, to better understand their revolutionary impact and even, obviously, go beyond Marx himself on the subject.

This deficiency of modern ecology makes it easier for it to be taken over by the vulgar economics that is in a dominant position in the contemporary world. This takeover is already under way, even well advanced.

Political environmentalism, like that proposed by Alain Lipietz, was first found in the ranks of the "pro-socialist" political left. Then the "green" movements (and after that, the green parties) were classed as center left, because of their expressed sympathies for social and international justice, their criticism of "waste," and their empathy with the workers and the "poor" populations. But, apart from the diversity of these movements, none of them had established a rigorous relationship between the authentic socialist dimension necessary to respond to the challenge and the no less necessary ecological dimension. To be able to do so, the distinction between value and wealth, as originated by Marx, cannot be ignored.

The takeover of environmentalism by vulgar ideology operates on two levels: by reducing the calculation in use value to an "improved" calculation of exchange value and also by integrating the ecological challenge into a "consensus" ideology. Both of these operations prevent a lucid awareness of the fact that ecological awareness and capitalism are antagonistic in their very essence. Vulgar economics has been capturing ecological calculation by leaps and bounds. Thousands of younger researchers, in the United States and, by imitation, in Europe, have been mobilized for that purpose. The "ecological costs" are thus assimilated to the externalities. The common method of cost-benefit analysis for measuring the exchange value (which itself is confused with the market price) is thus used to arrive at a "fair price," integrating the external economies and the "diseconomies." And the trick is done!

In fact, as we can already see, the oligopolies have taken over environmentalism to justify opening up new fields for their destructive expansion. François Houtart has given an excellent example in his book on agrofuels. (François Houtart, *Agrofuels: Big Profits, Ruined Lives and Human Ecological Destruction,* (London: Pluto Books, 2010.)

Green capitalism is now the order of the day for those in power in the Triad (right and left) and the directors of oligopolies. The environmentalism in question, of course, conforms to "weak sustainability"—to use the current jargon—that is, the marketing of rights of access to the planet's resources. All the conventional economists have openly rallied to this position, proposing the auctioning of world resources (fisheries, pollution permits, etc.).

This is a proposition which simply supports the oligopolies in their ambition to mortgage the future of the peoples of the South still further.

This capture of the environmentalist discourse is providing a very useful service to imperialism. It makes it possible to marginalize, if not to eliminate, the development issue. As we know, the question of development was not on the international agenda until the countries of the South were able to impose it by their own initiatives, forcing the powers of the Triad to negotiate and make concessions. But once the Bandung era was over, it was no longer a question of development, but only of opening up the markets. And ecology, as it is interpreted by the dominant powers, is just prolonging this state of affairs.

The taking over of environmental discourse through consensus politics (the necessary expression of the concept of end-of-history capitalism) is no less advanced. This capture has had an easy passage, for it responds to the alienations and illusions on which the dominant culture feeds, which is that of capitalism. It has been easy because this culture really does exist, is in place and dominant in the minds of most human beings, in the South as well as in the North.

In contrast, it is difficult to express the needs of a socialist counter-culture. A socialist culture is not there, in front of us. It is the future and has to be invented, a civilization project, open to an inventive imaginary. Formulas like "socialization through democracy and not through the market" and "cultural dominance instead of economics, served by politics" are not enough, in spite of the success they have had in initiating the historical process of transformation. For it will be a long secular process: the reconstruction of societies on principles other than those of capitalism, both in the North and in the South, cannot be rapid. But the construction of the future, even if it is far off, starts today.

Audacity, More Audacity

The historical circumstances created by the implosion of contemporary capitalism require the radical left, in the North as well as the South, to be bold in formulating its political alternative to the existing system.

Why audacity? Contemporary capitalism is a capitalism of generalized monopolies, whose most important characteristics have been described in the initial pages of this book. Under these conditions monopoly capital has openly declared war on workers and peoples. This declaration is formulated in the sentence "Liberalism is not negotiable." Monopoly capital will definitely continue its wild ride and not slow down. The criticism of "regulation" that I make below is grounded in this fact. We are not living in a historical moment in which the search for a "social compromise" is a possible option. There have been such moments in the past, such as the postwar social compromise between capital and labor specific to the social-democratic state in the West, the actually existing socialism in the East, and the popular national projects of the South. But our present historical moment is not the same. So the conflict is between monopoly capital and workers and people who are invited to an unconditional surrender. Defensive strategies of resistance under these conditions are ineffective and bound to be eventually defeated. In the face of war declared by monopoly capital, workers and peoples must develop strategies that allow them to take the offensive.The period of social war is necessarily accompanied by the proliferation of international political conflicts and military interventions of the imperialist powers of the Triad. The strategy of "military control of the planet" by the armed forces of the United States and its subordinate NATO allies is ultimately the only means by which the imperialist monopolies of the Triad can expect to continue their domination over the peoples, nations, and the states of the South.

Faced with this challenge of the war declared by the monopolies, what alternatives are being proposed?

*First response: "market regulation" (financial and otherwise).*These are initiatives that monopolies and governments claim they are pursuing. It is only empty rhetoric, designed to mislead public opinion. These initiatives cannot stop the mad rush for financial return that is the result of the logic of accumulation controlled by monopolies. They are therefore a false alternative.

Second response: a return to the postwar models. These responses feed a triple nostalgia: (1) the rebuilding of a true "social democracy" in the West; (2) the resurrection of "socialisms" founded on the principles that governed those of the twentieth century; (3) the return to formulas of popular nationalism in the peripheries of the South. These nostalgias imagine it is possible to "roll back" monopoly capitalism, forcing it to regress to what it was in 1945. But history never allows such returns to the past. Capitalism must be confronted as it is today, not as what we would have wished it to be by imagining the blocking of its evolution. However, these longings continue to haunt large segments of the left throughout the world.

Third response: the search for a "humanist" consensus. I define this pious wish in the following way: the illusion that a consensus among fundamentally conflicting interests would be possible. Naïve ecology movements, among others, share this illusion.

Fourth response: the illusions of the past. These illusions invoke "specificity" and "right to difference" without bothering to understand their scope and meaning. The past has already answered the questions for the future. These "culturalisms" can take many para-religious or ethnic forms. Theocracies and ethnocracies become convenient substitutes for the democratic social struggles that have been evacuated from their agenda.

Fifth response: priority of "personal freedom." The range of responses based on this priority, considered the exclusive "supreme value," includes in its ranks the diehards of "representative electoral democracy," which is equated with democracy itself. The formula separates the democratization of societies from social progress, and even tolerates a de facto association with social regression in order not to risk discrediting democracy, now reduced to the status of a tragic farce. But there are even more dangerous forms of this position. I refer here to some common "postmodernist" currents by commentators (Toni Negri in particular) who imagine that the individual has already become the subject of history, as if communism, which will allow the individual to be emancipated from alienation and actually become the subject of history, were already here.

It is clear that all of the responses above, including those of the right (such as the "regulations" that do not affect private property monopolies) still find powerful echoes among a majority of the people on the left. The war declared by the generalized monopoly capitalism of contemporary imperialism has nothing to fear from the false alternatives I have just outlined.

So what is to be done? This moment offers us the historic opportunity to go much further; it demands as the only effective response a bold and audacious radicalization in the formulation of alternatives capable of moving workers and peoples to take the offensive to defeat their adversaries strategy of war. These formulations, based on the analysis of actually existing contemporary capitalism, must directly confront the future that is to be built, and ignore the nostalgia for the past and illusions of identity or consensus.

Audacious Programs for the Radical Left

I will organize the following general proposals under three headings: (1) socialize the ownership of monopolies; (2) de-financialize the management of the economy; (3) de-globalize international relations.

Socialize the Ownership of Monopolies

The effectiveness of the alternative response necessarily requires the questioning of the very principle of private property of monopoly capital. Proposing to "regulate" financial operations, to return markets to "transparency," to allow agents' expectations" to be "rational," and to define the terms of a consensus on these reforms without abolishing the private property of monopolies, is nothing other than throwing dust in the eyes of the naïve public. Monopolies are asked to "manage" reforms against their own interests, ignoring the fact that they retain a thousand and one ways to circumvent the objectives of such reforms.

The alternative social project should be to reverse the direction of the current social order (social disorder) produced by the strategies of monopolies to ensure maximum and stabilized employment, and to ensure decent wages growing in parallel with the productivity of social labor. This objective is simply impossible without the expropriation of the power of monopolies.

The "software of economic theorists" (in the words of François Morin) must be reconstructed. The absurd and impossible economic theory of "expectations" expels democracy from the management of economic decision making. Audacity in this instance requires radical reform of education for the training not only of economists but also of all those called to occupy management positions. Monopolies are institutional bodies that must be managed according to the principles of democracy, in direct conflict with those who sanctify private property. Although the term "commons," imported from the Anglo-Saxon world, is itself ambiguous because it is always disconnected from the debate on the meaning of social conflicts (Anglo-Saxon language deliberately ignores the reality of social classes), the term could be invoked specifically to call monopolies part of the commons. The abolition of the private owner-ship of monopolies takes place through their nationalization. This first legal action is unavoidable. But audacity here means going beyond that step to propose plans for the socialization of the management of nation-alized monopolies and the promotion of the democratic social struggles that are engaged on this long road.

I will give here a concrete example of what could be involved in plans of socialization.

"Capitalist" farmers (those of developed countries), like "peasant" farmers (mostly in the South), are all prisoners of both the upstream monopolies that provide inputs and credit, and the downstream ones on which they depend for processing, transportation, and marketing of their products. Therefore they have no real autonomy in their "decisions." In addition the productivity gains they make are siphoned off by the monop-olies that have reduced producers to the status of "subcontractors." What possible alternative?

Public institutions working within a legal framework that would set the mode of governance must replace the monopolies. These would be constituted of representatives of (1) farmers (the principal interests); (2) upstream units (manufacturers of inputs, banks) and downstream (food industry, retail chains); (3) consumers; (4) local authorities (interested in natural and social environments—schools, hospitals, urban planning and housing, transportation); and (5) the state (citizens). Representatives of these components would be self-selected according to procedures con-sistent with their own mode of socialized management, such as units of production of inputs that are themselves managed by directorates of workers directly employed by the units as well as those who are employed by subcontracting units and so on. These structures should be designed by formulas that associate management personnel with each of these levels, such as research centers for scientific, independent and appropriate tech-nology. We could even conceive of a representation of capital providers (the small shareholders) inherited from the nationalization, if deemed useful. The proposed procedure would abolish the position of power through which the monopolies exploit workers and subcontractors by means of the price structures imposed on them. In its place would be a power founded on social solidarity, and truly just prices structured on the basis of equal rates of profit for all enterprises. This system would thus allow a different development. A more effective and more rational development path, because it would answer to society's collective choices, would bring the whole productive system onto the path of progress, and would stave off the destructive effects characteristic of monopoly capitalism. This is a state-capitalist model designed to be open to evolving in ways governed by a socialist perspective: it should be regarded as the form of "market socialism" required at the current stage. Obviously this procedure implies abolishing the principle that shareholder value should be maximized, the principle that underlies financialization that serves the interests of the generalized monopolies alone.

We are therefore talking about institutional approaches that are more complex than the forms of "self-directed" or "cooperative" that we have known. Ways of working need to be invented that allow the exercise of genuine democracy in the management of the economy, based on open negotiation among all interested parties. A formula is required that systematically links the democratization of society with social progress, in contrast with the reality of capitalism that dissociates democracy, which is reduced to the formal management of politics, from social conditions abandoned to the "market" dominated by what monopoly capital produces. Then and only then can we talk about true transparency of markets, regulated in institutionalized forms of socialized management.

The example may seem marginal in the developed capitalist countries because farmers there are a very small proportion of workers (3 to 7 percent). However, this issue is central to the South where the rural population will remain significant for some time. Here access to land, which must be guaranteed for all (with the least possible inequality of access) is fundamental to principles advancing peasant agriculture (I refer here to my previous work on this question). "Peasant agriculture" should not be understood as synonymous with "stagnant agriculture" or "traditional and *folklorique*." The necessary progress of peasant agriculture does require some "modernization," although this term is a misnomer because it immediately suggests to many modernization through capitalism. More effective inputs, credits, and production and supply chains are necessary to improve the productivity of peasant labor. The formulas proposed here pursue the objective of enabling this modernization in ways and in a spirit that is "non-capitalist," that is to say, grounded in a socialist perspective.

Obviously the specific example chosen here is one that needs to be institutionalized. The nationalization/socialization of the management of monopolies in the sectors of industry and transport, banks, and other financial institutions should be imagined in the same spirit, while taking into account the specificities of their economic and social functions in the constitution of their directorates. Again these directorates should involve the workers in the company as well as those of subcontractors, representatives of upstream industries, banks, research institutions, consumers, and citizens.

The nationalization/socialization of monopolies addresses a fundamental need at the central axis of the challenge confronting workers and peoples under contemporary capitalism of generalized monopolies. It is the only way to stop the accumulation by dispossession that is driving the management of the economy by the monopolies. Indeed, the accumulation dominated by monopolies can only reproduce itself if the area subject to "market management" is constantly expanding. This is achieved by excessive privatization of public services (dispossession of citizens) and access to natural resources (dispossession of peoples). The extraction of profit of "independent" economic units by the monopolies is even a dispossession (of capitalists!) by the financial oligarchy.

The challenge that would face us once we enter the long road to communism can perhaps be summed up thusly: how are we to socialize "large-scale production" involving many collectives (themselves also large) of social labor—entities that, moreover, interact among themselves at local, national, and global levels? In my opinion, one thing is certain: history has no reverse gear. It simply cannot be imagined that production by individual artisans and by small local collectives might replace large-scale productive operations, the very basis for full deployment of the scientific and technological capabilities descended from those initiated—albeit barely so—by capitalism. The proposition that I have advanced by way of example tries to answer that central question. To reject this proposition on the pretext that it involves defining a political strategy to be carried out by a "party" (or a collective of parties and social organizations) comes down to believing that spontaneity alone can accomplish whatever is required.

And then, how to go further? For, indeed, socialism is not an improved form of capitalism. In my writings I have put it this way: socialism is not a "capitalism without capitalists" but a higher level of civilization. The inescapable goals of revolutionary thought (Marxist, as I understand that term) are to eradicate all types of oppression caused by exploitation, as well as the sorts of alienation involved in their workings, and to abolish wage labor and the price mechanism. But I remain convinced that our road to that goal is very long and it is indispensable that we specify our intermediate strategic objectives.

In making these proposals I have respected our need to start from our present condition, and especially from present forms of large-scale production. The proposed methods of social reorganization have a single aim: to abolish the control of capital (the generalized monopolies) over those forms of production, initiating its replacement with forms of governance based on democracy and negotiated linkage among partners in the modern epoch's extended division of labor.

Nationalization/socialization of the monopolies: our response to the basic exigencies that form the central axis of the challenge confronting workers and peoples under contemporary generalized-monopoly capitalism. It alone would make it possible to end the process of accumulation through dispossession dictated by the logic of economic governance by the monopolies. This formulation seeks not to define a possible organic constitution for the coming communist society. It is simply the response to the immediate challenge of escaping from capitalism through construction of a first stage in the long socialist transition. This socialism would have, as Marx said, barely emerged from "the womb of capitalism"—and its formulation shows the marks of its birth. Nevertheless, because it is based on abolition of the capitalist monopolies' property, it counts, for me, as a revolutionary advance that through democratic discussions would prepare the ground for further advances on the long road to communism.

De-Financialization: A World without Wall Street

Nationalization/socialization of monopolies would in and of itself abolish the principle of "shareholder value" imposed by the strategy of accumulation in the service of monopoly rents. This objective is essential for any bold agenda to escape the ruts in which the management of today's economy is mired. Its implementation pulls the rug out from under the feet of the financialization of economic governance. Are we returning to the famous "euthanasia of the rentier" advocated by Keynes in his time? Not necessarily, and certainly not completely. Savings can be encouraged by financial reward, but on condition that their origin (household savings of workers, businesses, communities) and their conditions of earnings are precisely defined. The discourse on macroeconomic savings in conventional economic theory hides the organization of exclusive access to the capital market of the monopolies. The so-called market-driven remuneration is then nothing other than the means to guarantee the growth of monopoly rents.

Of course, the nationalization/socialization of monopolies also applies to banks, at least the major ones. But the socialization of their intervention (credit policies) has specific characteristics that require an appropriate design in the constitution of their directorates. Nationalization in the classical sense of the term implies only the substitution of the state for the boards of directors formed by private shareholders. This would permit, in principle, implementation of bank credit policies formulated by the State—which is no small thing. But it is certainly not sufficient when we consider that socialization requires the direct participation in the management of the bank by the relevant social partners. Here the "self-management" of banks by their staff would not be appropriate. The staff concerned should certainly be involved in decisions about their working conditions, but little else, because it is not their place to determine the credit policies to be implemented.

If the directorates must deal with the conflicts of interest of those that provide loans (the banks) and those who receive them (the enterprises), the formula for the composition of directorates must be designed taking into account what the enterprises are and what they require: a restructuring of the banking system, which has become overly centralized since the regulatory frameworks of the past two centuries were abandoned over the past four decades. There is a strong argument to justify the reconstruction of banking specialization according to the requirements of the recipients of their credit as well as their economic function (provision of short-term liquidity, contributing to the financing of investments in the medium and long term). We could then, for example, create an "agriculture bank" (or a coordinated ensemble of agriculture banks) whose clientele is composed not only of farmers and peasants but also those involved in the "upstream and downstream" of agriculture described above. The bank's directorate would involve the "bankers" (staff officers of the bank, who would have been recruited by the directorate) and clients (farmers or peasants, and other upstream and downstream entities).

We can imagine other sets of articulated banking systems, appropriate to various industrial sectors, in which the directorates would involve the industrial clients, centers of research and technology and services, to ensure control of the ecological impact of the industry, thus ensuring minimal risk (while recognizing that no human action is completely without risk), and subject to transparent democratic debate.

The de-financialization of economic management would also require two sets of legislation. The first concerns the authority of a sovereign state to ban speculative fund (hedge funds) operations in its territory. The second concerns pension funds, which are now major operators in the financialization of the economic system. These funds were designed— first in the United States, of course—to transfer to employees the risks normally incurred by capital, the very risks invoked to justify capital's remuneration! So this is a scandalous arrangement, in clear contradiction even with the ideological defense of capitalism. But this "invention" is an ideal instrument for the strategies of accumulation dominated by monopolies.

The abolition of pension funds is necessary for the benefit of distributive pension systems, which by their very nature require and allow democratic debate to determine the amounts and periods of assessment and the relationship between the amounts of pensions and remuneration paid. In a democracy that respects social rights, these pension systems are universally available to all workers. However, at a pinch, and so as not to prohibit what a group of individuals might desire to put in place, supplementary pension funds could be allowed.

All measures of de-financialization suggested here lead to an obvious conclusion: "a world without Wall Street," to borrow the title of the book by François Morin, is possible and desirable. In a world without Wall Street, the economy is still largely controlled by the "market." But these markets are for the first time truly transparent, regulated by democratic negotiation among genuine social partners (for the first time they are no longer adversaries as they are necessarily under capitalism). It is the financial "market"—opaque by nature and subjected to the requirements of management for the benefit of the monopolies—that is abolished. We could even explore whether it would be useful or not to shut down the stock exchanges, given that the rights to property, both in its private as well as social form, would be conducted differently. We could even consider whether the stock exchange could be reestablished to this new end. The symbol in any case—"a world without Wall Street"—nevertheless retains its power.

De-financialization certainly does not mean the abolition of macroeconomic policy and in particular the macro management of credit. On the contrary it restores its efficiency by freeing it from its subjugation to the strategies of rent-seeking monopolies. The restoration of the powers of national central banks, no longer "independent" but dependent on both the state and markets regulated by the democratic negotiation of social partners, gives the formulation of macro credit policy its effectiveness in the service of socialized management of the economy.

At the International Level: De-Linking

I use here the term "de-linking" that I proposed half a century ago, a term that contemporary discourse appears to have replaced with the synonym "de-globalization." I have never conceptualized de-linking as an autarkic retreat, but rather as a strategic reversal in the face of both internal and external forces in response to the unavoidable requirements of self-determined development. De-linking promotes the reconstruction of a globalization based on negotiation, rather than submission to the exclusive interests of the imperialist monopolies. It also makes possible the reduction of international inequalities.

De-linking is necessary because the measures advocated in the two previous sections can never really be implemented at the global scale, or even at a regional level (for example, Europe). They can only be initiated in the context of states/nations with advanced radical social and political struggles, committed to a process of socialization of the management of their economy. Imperialism, in the form that it took until just after the Second World War, created the contrast between industrialized imperialist centers and dominated peripheries where industry was prohibited. The victories of national liberation movements began the process of the industrialization of the peripheries, through the implementation of delinking policies required for the option of self-reliant development. Associated with social reforms that were at times radical, these de-linkings created the conditions for the eventual "emergence" of those countries that had gone furthest in this direction—China leading the pack, of course.

But the imperialism of the current era, the imperialism of the Triad, forced to retreat and adjust itself to the conditions of this new era, rebuilt itself on new foundations, based on "advantage" by which it sought to hold on to the privilege of exclusivity that I have classified in five categories. The control of:

- technology;
- access to natural resources of the planet;
- global integration of the monetary and financial system;
- systems of communication and information;
- weapons of mass destruction.

The main form of de-linking today is thus defined precisely by the challenge to these five privileges of contemporary imperialism. Emerging countries are engaged in de-linking from these five privileges, with varying degrees of control and self-determination, of course. Though earlier success over the past two decades in de-linking enabled countries to accelerate their development, in particular through industrial development within the globalized "liberal" system using "capitalist" means, this success has fueled delusions about the possibility of continuing on this path, that is to say, emerging as new "equal capitalist partners." The attempt to co-opt the most prestigious of these countries with the creation of the G20 has encouraged these illusions.

But with the current ongoing implosion of the imperialist system (called globalization), these illusions are likely to dissipate. The conflict between the imperialist powers of the Triad and emerging countries is already visible, and is expected to worsen. If they want to move forward, the societies of emerging countries will be forced to turn more toward self-reliant modes of development through national plans and by strengthening South-South cooperation.

Audacity, under such circumstances, involves engaging vigorously and coherently toward this end, bringing together the required measures of delinking with the desired advances in social progress. The goal of this radicalization is threefold: the democratization of society; the consequent social progress achieved; and the taking of anti-imperialist positions. A commitment to this direction is possible, not only for societies in emerging countries but also in the "abandoned" or the "written-off" countries of the global South. These countries had been effectively re-colonized through the structural adjustment programs of the 1980s. Their peoples are now in open revolt, whether they have already scored victories (South America) or not (in the Arab world). Audacity here means that the radical left in these societies must have the courage to take the measure of the challenges they face and to support the continuation and radicalization of the necessary struggles that are in progress.

The de-linking of the South prepares the way for the deconstruction of the imperialist system itself. This is particularly apparent in areas affected by the management of the global monetary and financial system, since it is the result of the hegemony of the dollar. But beware: it is an illusion to expect to substitute for this system "another world monetary and financial system" that is better balanced and favorable to the development of the peripheries. As always, the search of a "consensus" over international reconstruction from above is mere wishful thinking akin to waiting for a miracle. What is on the agenda now is the deconstruction of the existing system—its implosion—and reconstruction of national alternative systems (for countries or continents or regions), as some projects in South America have already begun. Audacity here is to have the courage to move forward with the strongest determination possible, without too much worry about the reaction of imperialism.

This same problematic of de-linking/dismantling is also of relevance to Europe, which is a subset of globalization dominated by monopolies. The European project was designed from the outset and built systematically to dispossess its peoples from their ability to exercise their democratic power. The European Union was established as a protectorate of the monopolies. With the implosion of the Eurozone, its submission to the will of the monopolies has resulted in the abolishment of democracy, which has been reduced to the status of farce and takes on extreme forms, namely focused on only one question: How are the "market" (that is to say monopolies) and the "rating agencies" (that is to say, again, the monopolies) reacting? How the people might react is no longer given the slightest consideration. It is thus obvious that here too there is no alternative to audacity: "disobeying" the rules imposed by the "European Constitution" and the imaginary central bank of the euro. In other words, there is no alternative to deconstruct the institutions of Europe and the Eurozone. This is the unavoidable prerequisite for the eventual reconstruction of "another Europe" of peoples and nations.

Audacity, More Audacity, Always Audacity

What I mean by audacity is therefore,

- for the radical left in the societies of the imperialist Triad, the need for an engagement in the building an alternative anti-monopoly social coalition.
- For the radical left in the societies of the peripheries, it is the need to engage in the building of an alternative anti-comprador social coalition.

It will take time to make progress in building these coalitions, but it could well accelerate if the radical left takes on movement with determination and engages in making progress on the long road of socialism. It is therefore necessary to propose strategies not "out of the crisis of capitalism," but "out of capitalism in crisis" to borrow from the title of one of my recent works.

We are in a crucial period in history. The only legitimacy of capitalism is to have created the conditions for passing on to socialism, understood as a higher stage of civilization. Capitalism is now an obsolete system, its continuation leading only to barbarism. No other capitalism is possible. The outcome of a clash of civilizations is, as always, uncertain. Either the radical left will succeed through the audacity of its initiatives to make revolutionary advances, or the counterrevolution will win. There is no effective compromise between these two responses to the challenge.

All the strategies of the non-radical left are in fact non-strategies; they are merely day-to-day adjustments to the vicissitudes of the imploding system. And if the powers that be want, like il gattopardo (the Leopard), to "change everything so that nothing changes," the candidates of the left believe it is possible to change life without touching the power of monopolies. The non-radical left will not stop the triumph of capitalist barbarism. They have already lost the battle for lack of wanting to take it on.

Audacity is what is necessary to bring about the autumn of capitalism that will be announced by the implosion of its system and by the birth of an authentic spring of the peoples, a spring that is possible.

REFERENCES

Samir Amin, *Ending the Crisis of Capitalism or Ending Capitalism?* (Oxford: Pambazuka, 2010), esp. "The Two Long Crises of Monopoly Capitalism," "Collective Imperialism," "The Three Forms of the System Taken in the Postwar Period," and "Accumulation through Dispossession."
Samir Amin, *L'éveil du Sud, l'ère de Bandoung* (Paris: Le temps des cerises, 2008). An analysis of the paths taken by the popular national experiences of the period.
Samir Amin, *From Capitalism to Civilisation: Reconstructing the Socialist Perspective* (Delhi: Tulika Books, 2010), esp. "Generalized Monopoly Capitalism," "The European Project and Social Movements."
Samir Amin, *Beyond U.S. Hegemony, Assessing the Prospects for a Multipolar World* (London: Zed, 2006).
Elmar Altvater, "The Plagues of Capitalism, Energy Crisis, Climate Collapse, Hunger and Financial Instabilities," paper presented to the World Forum for Alternatives, Caracas, 2008.
François Houtart, *Agrofuels: Big Profits, Ruined Lives and Human Ecological Destruction* (London: Pluto Books, 2010).

On China, the South, and Europe

Samir Amin, *The Liberal Virus* (London: Pluto, 2004), esp. "The Ideology of Consensus."
Samir Amin, *The Law of Worldwide Value* (New York: Monthly Review Press, 2010).
Aurélien Bernier, *Désobéissons à l'Union Européenne* (Paris: Les mille et une nuits, 2011).
Jacques Nikonoff, *Sortir de l'euro* (Paris: Les mille et une nuits, 2011).
François Morin, *Un Monde sans Wall Street* (Paris: Le seuil, 2011).

CONCLUSION

IN THIS BOOK I HAVE suggested analyses articulated around my central definition of generalized-monopoly capitalism. It is this concept that allows us to put in their right place, and accord significance to, all the striking new facts that, in all regions (both central and peripheral) of the world, characterize contemporary capitalism. It makes coherent a painting that otherwise would appear to be random and chaotic.

Monopoly capitalism first took form at the end of the nineteenth century, but it only crystallized as a system in the United States in the 1920s. It then took over Europe and Japan in the "Thirty Glorious" postwar years. The concept of surplus, advanced by Paul Sweezy and Paul Baran during the 1950s, lets us grasp the essence of how capitalism was qualitatively transformed by the monopolies' rise to dominance. I was immediately convinced by this work that enriched the Marxist critique of capitalism, and in the 1970s I began to reformulate it. This, in my opinion, required analyzing the transformation of the primary (1920–1970) monopoly capitalism into generalized-monopoly capitalism as a qualitatively new phase of the system.

My first reformulation of generalized-monopoly capitalism goes back to 1978 when I proposed an interpretation of capital's response to the challenge of its new long systemic crisis, which had begun in the 1971–75 period. In that interpretation I emphasized three aspects of that anticipated response: reinforced centralization of the monopolies' control over the economy, deepening of globalization and of the outsourcing of manufacturing toward the peripheries, and financialization. A book that I and

André Gunder Frank wrote together in 1978, *N'attendons pas 1984* (Don't Wait for 1984), went unnoticed, probably because our theses were ahead of their time. But today those three characteristics have become blindingly clear to everyone.

We needed to give a name to this new phase of monopoly capitalism. What about "late monopoly capitalism"? I thought that this adjective, a bit like the prefix "post," had to be avoided because it gave no positive sense of what was new, its content and importance. But the adjective "generalized" specifies rightly: the monopolies were thenceforward in position to reduce all (or almost all) economic actors to subcontractor status. The example of family farming in the capitalist centers, which I have discussed in this book, is the best example of that.

This concept of generalized-monopoly capitalism enables us to specify the scope of the major transformations involving the configuration of class structures and the ways in which political life is managed. In the centers of the system, the United States/Western Europe/Japan Triad, generalized-monopoly capitalism brought about the generalization of the wage system. The managers, termed "executives," involved in the monopolies' administration of the economy, were thenceforward salaried employees. I have shown that they did not take part in the creation of surplus-value but became consumers of it, and therefore they came to make up a constituent part of the bourgeoisie. At society's other pole the generalized proletarianization suggested by the wage system was accompanied by multiplication of the ways in which the labor force was segmented. In other words, the "proletariat" (in its historic form) was disappearing at the very moment when proletarianization was becoming generalized. In the peripheral countries—extremely diverse, as always, since they are linked only by a negative definition (as regions that are not constituted as centers of the global system)—the effects of their domination (indirect control) by generalized-monopoly capital are no less obvious. Above the diversity of local ruling classes and varying statuses of subordinate classes stands the power of a dominant super-class emergent in the wake of globalization. This super-class is sometimes mainly made up of comprador corruptionists, sometimes mainly of a political class ensconced in party-state rule, often of a mixture of the two.

Generalized-monopoly capitalism's economic dominance, in turn, both demanded and enabled transformation of the forms through which political life was administered. In the central countries a new "consensus" political culture (perhaps seeming superficial, but nevertheless having real effects), amounting to depoliticization, took the place of a previous political culture based on a left-right contestation that gave meaning to bourgeois democracy and served to contain class-struggle contradictions within its framework. The market, that is, the "non-market" reality marking the generalized monopolies' administration of the economy, and "democracy" are so far from being synonymous as to be antinomies. In the peripheral countries the monopolization of power by the dominant local super-class referred to above likewise involves the negation of democracy. Which in turn fortifies forms of depoliticization, forms seemingly diverse yet identical in their effects. Wang Hui has provided a superb analysis of this in regard to contemporary China (since the 1989 Tiananmen Square repression). I have tried to do likewise in regard to those countries victimized by the rise of political Islam.

My suggestion is that we go one step further in our analysis of generalized-monopoly capitalism by calling it the triumph of "abstract capitalism." In the perfected form that it attained with the Industrial Revolution and its extension during the nineteenth century, capitalism corresponded to a concrete historical reality that in its decisive dimensions was adapted to the logic of its *modus operandi*. The economic future's new master class, steadily rising to the rank of political ruling class, was made up of men and families attached to well-defined economic entities; they were the owners of the predominant capital of their own factories, trading houses, and financial firms. They made up a "concrete bourgeoisie" that directly through their private properties took charge of economic management. It was management through effective competition among capitals (and thus among capitalists, among the bourgeois). It was on an understanding of this concrete competition that Marx's analysis of the transformation of the value system into a price system was based. Finally, on the level of macroeconomic management, the organizing principle enabling them to transcend the chaos of competition operated through a concrete commodity money—gold. This administration of capitalism's collective interests, transcending those of particular capitalists. operated (ideally through bourgeois democracy) in the political framework of a national state—which thus guaranteed coherence of national political management with the needs of capital accumulation.

Today, in every one of these crucial respects, the reality is quite otherwise. What is concrete vanishes, giving way to an abstract reproduction of capital.

The fragmented, and thereby concrete, economic power of bourgeois proprietors gives way to centralized power in the hands of the directors of the monopolies and their salaried administrative staffs. Generalized-monopoly capitalism involves not just the concentration of property (which, on the contrary, is more dispersed than ever) but control over its administration. This is why it would be deceptive to insert the adjective "patrimonial" into the phrase "contemporary capitalism." Stockholders, supposed to rule, seem to have power. However, the real sovereigns, who make all the decisions in their name, are the directors of the monopolies. Such administration, in turn, obviates the former *modus operandi* of competition that used to be the regulatory mechanism for capital accumulation. Instead we get a system of management based on alternation between negotiated cooperation and brutal conflict among monopolies, using methods that are not at all those of a pretended "fair and open competition." Power, in the most abstract sense of the word, replaces concrete effective competition. Moreover, the deepening globalization of the system undoes the holistic (simultaneously economic, political, and social) logic of national systems leaving in its place no global logic whatsoever. This is (as per the title of my book published in 2001 and since adopted by others) the "empire of chaos." In actuality international political violence has taken the place of economic competition, even though in rhetoric it is claimed that it is competition that regulates the system.

For the theory of value this evolutionary path of the capitalist system is problematic.

It was in the epoch of competitive capitalism, the nineteenth century, that Marx composed his critique of capitalism and of the economic theory legitimizing its extension. The theory of value and that of the transformation of the value system into a price system made up the central axis of that critique. The bourgeois economists preceding Marx (those, like Bastiat, whom he called "vulgar economists" in distinction from figures like Quesnay, Smith, and Ricardo) and above all those following him put their effort into demonstrating that subordinating society to the development-requirements of generalized competitive markets would result in a "general equilibrium" favoring progress in every nation and in the world as a whole. The two great attempts at a proof of this by Walras and Sraffa failed, as I pointed out in my book *The Law of Worldwide Value*. Moreover, the reality of the global system has proven that capitalism would result, not in homogenization of economic conditions on that scale, but in its opposite, ever-growing polarization.

A half-century ago, Baran and Sweezy showed that the abolition of competition (or at least the radical transformation of that word's meaning, its workings, and its outcomes) by the monopolies had disconnected the price system from its foundation, the value system. The monopoly system hid, yet without erasing, the referential framework that used to define capitalist rationality.

This loss of basic referential points (values) was concomitant with abandonment of historic capitalism's other solid referential point—commodity money (metallic gold). Gold was given up progressively, starting with the chaos of the First World War. An attempted return to gold in the interwar years malfunctioned. The Bretton Woods solution (1945–71) worked only insofar as the United States took on the function of economic hegemon (the gold-exchange standard—with the dollar exchangeable for gold between central banks at a fixed rate, making it equivalent to gold), and it disappeared when Nixon ended international convertibility of the dollar in 1971. Ever since then, floating exchange rates have furnished yet another cause of permanent chaos.

In 1957 and again in 1973, I sketched out a critique of the logic of accumulation as transformed by loss of the reference point that had been provided by metallic money. This loss of a reference point involved the appearance of a new way to manage accumulation, linked to the inflationary disorder that thenceforward had become possible. Currently, the affirmation of a will to abolish inflation from the outlook (without, for all that, returning to metallic money) through the workings of permanently "deflationist" monetary policies (a will affirmed more strongly by Germany than elsewhere) calls on us to revisit and deepen our analysis of the concept of money under capitalism. Losing sight of the solid referential point that was metallic money might have been compensated for through centralized management of credit by the state. This solution was partly effectuated during the postwar "Thirty Glorious Years" (1945–75). The onset of systemic crisis in 1975 evoked a deepening of globalization in response (and, for Europe, the construction of a European system within that globalization framework). This led to abandoning the state's administration of credit and yielding it to the direct power of the monopolies. But the resulting stagnation and chaos put the goldbugs back in the saddle, showing that economistic alienation and the permanence of an indispensable fetish are inseparable from each other.

The abstract character of contemporary capitalism is thus synonymous with permanent, insurmountable, chaos. By its very nature capitalist accumulation has always been synonymous with "disorder" in Marx's sense of the word: a system forced from disequilibrium to disequilibrium (under the impulsion of class struggles and of conflicts among the powers) without ever showing a tendency toward equilibrium. But thanks to the effective nature of competition among fragmented capitals, to state management of the productive system in a national framework, and to policies respectful of the requirements of maintaining a metallic money, that disorder was contained within reasonable limits. With the advent of contemporary abstract capitalism those boundaries disappeared, making the swings from disequilibrium to disequilibrium more violent.

Bourgeois economic theory endeavors to respond to the challenge—by denying its existence. To that end it just goes on with its conventional rhetoric, talking of (nonexistent) "fair and open competition" and of "true prices." We have seen in the agriculture example that those "true prices" make farmers work without any compensation except for what they receive in the form of public subsidies. They talk of a "diminished state" even though the public sector's share of GDP not only has never been so large—and so absolutely essential to the survival of the system. But in parallel to this empty and fantastical rhetoric is a supposed theoretical rehabilitation of the (false) theorem of market self-regulation: analysis of economic decision making, attributed without any proof to the behavior of "individuals," is now shifted to their "expectations." And so the circle is closed: economic theory goes on describing an imaginary system (and not the actual capitalist system) and, what is more, in a fashion that explains anything and everything by way of "expectations" whose degree of conformity to reality is unknowable to the "expecters" themselves. More than ever economic theory has become ideological rhetoric (in the most bluntly negative sense of the term) whose objective is to make us accept whatever is decided by the sole deciders: the generalized monopolies.

The aim of this book was simply to analyze the reality of contemporary globalized-monopoly capitalism. And, by that very fact, to show that this system cannot survive and that its now ongoing implosion is an inevitability. It is in this sense that contemporary capitalism deserves the adjective *senile* that I have applied to it: we are in the autumn of capitalism.

It was not my intention to go further and to suggest strategies of political action enabling the construction of a positive alternative. To take up that challenge would have required examination of fundamental questions not approached in this book, notably that of the subjective factors, the active elements, of society. So I have limited myself, in the final chapter, to sketching out the broad lines of challenges that cannot be taken up except on one condition—the reconstitution of audacious radical leftist movements. Then and only then can the autumn of capitalism coincide with the springtime of the peoples.

Such is not (yet?) the case. The only thing I ascertain is the expected implosion (or perhaps the explosion) of the system. It shows itself in the revolts of the South's peoples (in Latin America, in the Arab world, and elsewhere), the rising conflicts between the emergent countries and the centers of the historic imperialist Triad, the implosion of the European system, and the rise of new struggles in the centers themselves. All of these are omens of potential repoliticization, which is itself the precondition for the rebirth, if it rises to the challenge, of the radical left.

INDEX

Hiferding, Rudolf, 26, 107
Hobson, John A., 26, 107
Hollande, François, 101
Houtart, François, 132
Hui, Wang, 151
humanism, 135
Hussein, Saddam, 54

immaterial production, *see* nonmaterial production
immigration and emigration, 110, 122, 129
imperialism: capitalism and, 8; central and peripheral countries created by, 144; Lenin on, 112; local ruling classes under, 30; peripheral countries' challenges to, 113–17; of Triad, 93–94
imperialist rents, 15, 20–21, 113–14, 120
independent contractors, 32
India, 47, 73; China compared with, 75
individualism, 11
Industrial Revolution, 106, 108, 109, 151
inequalities, in China, 79
internationalism, 100, 103, 119–21
Iran, 48, 52–55, 62
Iraq, 54, 55, 59
Islam: in Egypt, 57, 61–63; in Iran, 53–54; political, 60–61, 63; in Turkey, 50
Ismail Pasha (Khedive, Egypt), 56
Israel, 55, 58, 59, 61
Italy, 90

Japan: atomic bombing of, 124; *see also* Triad

Kautsky, Karl, 67, 129
Kemalists, 50, 51
Keynes, John Maynard, 141
Khomeini (Ayatollah, Iran), 53–55
knowledge capitalism, 20
Korea, 79
Kuomintang (China), 77, 80

labor: simple, complex, and abstract, 22–23; *see also* social labor
Lagarde, 99
land: agrarian question and, 66–68; current agrarian question and, 127–31; enclosures of, 109; Marx on, 131; petty production and, 68–71
languages, 95
late monopoly capitalism, 150

Latin America, 91–92, 94; control over natural resources in, 117
Lenin, V.I.: on agrarian question, 66; on imperialism, 112; on monopoly capitalism, 26, 107, 108
liberal capitalism, 90
Lipietz, Alain, 132
lumpen-development, 10, 31; emergence and, 46–48; in peripheral countries, 33
Luxemburg, Rosa, 112

Maastricht Treaty, 92, 96, 97
Magdoff, Harry, 19
Maoism, 75
Mao Tse Tung, 66–68, 77; Cultural Revolution of, 81; on dimensions of reality, 114; governing philosophy of, 83
market regulation, 134
market socialism, 74
Marx, Karl, 151; on accumulation, 107; on disorder in capitalism, 154; on distinction between value and wealth, 131, 132; on market in capitalism, 28; on nationalization, 140; on productivity, 24; on proletariat, 31; on social labor, 14; on stages of development, 77; theory of value of, 152; two departments model by, 12, 18, 19
Marxism and Marxists, 113–17, 140; on agrarian question, 129; on surplus, 19
media clergy, 34–39
Mehmet El Fateh (sultan, Turkey), 48–49
Menderes, Adnan, 51
mercantilism, 106, 109–10, 122
Merkel, Angela, 102
Mexico, 92
middle classes, 32; in China, 83–84; in peripheral countries, 31
Ming dynasty (China), 106
Mitterand, François, 125
modernity, 109, 115
modernization, 129; in Iran, 53–54
Mohamed Ali, Pacha, 48
Mohammed Ali (viceroy, Egypt), 56
money, 153; *see also* currencies
monopolies, 36; generalized, 15–16; socializing ownership of, 136–40
monopoly capitalism, 26, 108, 149
Monroe Doctrine, 91
Morin, François, 136, 142
Mossadeqh, 53

social labor: abstract, 22; growth in productivity of, 17–18; Marx on, 14; productivity of, in nonmaterial production, 13
South Korea, 47
South Yemen Republic, 59
sovereignty, 102–3
Soviet Union: China compared with, 80–81; democratization of, 123–24; forced collectivization in, 66; Iran and, 53; outside world capitalist system, 74; Turkey and, 50
Spain, 90
Sraffa, 153
Stalin, Josef, 50, 66
state, 115–16
state capitalism, in China, 71–74
stock exchanges, 143
stockholders, 152
Stockholm Appeal, 124
Stockholm Conference (1972), 131
Sung dynasty (China), 106
Sunnis, 54
Sun Yat Sen, 77
surplus, 17–21, 149
surplus-value, production of, consumption of, 23–24
sustainable development, 131–33
Sweezy, Paul M., 19, 20, 149, 153
Syria, 55, 59

Taiping Revolution (China), 67, 77
Taiwan, 47, 79
Tanzimat (Turkey), 48, 49
taxes, 18
technology: agriculture dependent on, 127, 129; segmentation of proletariat and, 31
Third World: new agrarian question in, 127–29; *see also* emergence
Tibet, 82
Toudeh (Iran), 53

Touraine, Alain, 10
transnational (multinational) corporations, 26, 44
Triad (U.S., Europe, Japan), 111; centralization of capital in, 45; collective imperialism of, 93–94; emergence under control of, 46; financialization in, 16; globalized financial monopolies of, 36; as imperialist center, 30; petty production in, 68
Turkey, 48–52

United Kingdom, *see* Great Britain
United Nations, 82, 118, 124
United States: corporations financed in, 28; Europe compared with, 89, 91–92; imperialism of, 94; Iran and, 53, 54; political strategy of, 81–82; transnational corporations in, 26; *see also* Triad
use value, 131–33

Venice (Italy), 28
Vietnam, 47, 66

Wafd (Egypt), 57
wage-scale, 24–25
Wallerstein, Immanuel, 90
Walras, Léon, 153
Western Europe: Eastern Europe subordinate to, 91, 92; imperialism of, 93; *see also* Triad
women, in Iran, 53, 54
World Trade Organization, 129; agriculture under, 128–30

Young Turks (Turkey), 49
yuan (Chinese currency), 75

Zasulich, Vera, 77